Is This Love or Narcissism?

How to Identify, Understand and Recover from Manipulation, Gaslighting and Narcissist Abuse.

Relationship Self-Assessment Guide Included

Cassandra McBride

Special Bonus!

Want access to the below books for _free_?

Get **_Free_** Unlimited Access to both of my prior two books by subscribing to my fan base below!

Table of Contents

Introduction 5

Chapter 1: Understanding Narcissism.. 11

Chapter 2: Recognizing Narcissistic Patterns in Relationships.................. 23

Chapter 3: The Impact of Narcissism on Partners 38

Chapter 4: Relationship Self-Assessment Guide.. 59

Chapter 5: Breaking Free from Narcissistic Influence................................ 91

Chapter 6: Techniques to End the Gaslighting and Manipulative Tactics.... 104

Chapter 7: Exiting a Narcissistic Relationship for Good............................115

Chapter 8: Healing from Narcissist Abuse and Moving Forward............ 128

Conclusion.. 143

References: 149

Introduction

"You're too sensitive."

"It's all in your head."

"You're overreacting."

These are the jabs Sarah heard daily from her partner, David, as she found herself sinking deeper into a relationship riddled with manipulation, gaslighting, and emotional abuse. From the outside, their relationship seemed picture-perfect, but behind closed doors, Sarah endured a constant cycle of narcissistic abuse.

When Sarah first met David, she was instantly drawn to his charisma, intelligence, and seemingly endless supply of affection. He pursued her with a single-minded intensity, showering her with compliments, gifts, and grand romantic gestures. Sarah felt like she had finally found her soulmate, someone who understood and appreciated her in a way that no one else ever had.

In the early months of their relationship, David made Sarah feel like the center of his universe. He wanted to spend every waking moment with her, and he made grandiose plans for their future together. He told her that he had never felt this way about anyone before and that he couldn't imagine his life without her.

Sarah was swept off her feet by David's attentiveness and devotion. She began to prioritize him above everything else in her life, spending less time with her friends and family and more time catering to his needs and desires. She felt a deep sense of responsibility for his happiness and well-being, and worked tirelessly to be the perfect partner for him.

However, as time passed, David's behavior began to change drastically. At first, the shifts were subtle - a snide comment here, a passive-aggressive remark there. Sarah initially brushed these incidents off, telling herself that David was just stressed or having a bad day.

But as the weeks turned into months, David's criticism and belittlement became more overt and frequent. He began to nitpick Sarah's appearance, mocking her clothing choices and telling her that she needed to lose weight. He dismissed her accomplishments at work, claiming she had only succeeded because of her looks or her connections.

David also started to twist Sarah's words and use them against her. If she expressed a concern or frustration, he would accuse her of being too sensitive or overreacting. If she tried to assert her needs or boundaries, he would tell her that she was being selfish or unreasonable. Sarah found herself constantly second-guessing her own thoughts and feelings, wondering if **she** *was the problem in the relationship.*

The gaslighting and manipulation escalated to the point where Sarah began to question her own sanity. David would deny events that she clearly remembered, or accuse her of saying or doing things that she knew she hadn't. He would tell her that she was imagining things or that she was crazy, and she began to believe him.

Sarah found herself apologizing for things she hadn't done, taking responsibility for David's emotional outbursts and hurtful behavior. She walked on eggshells around him, never knowing what might trigger his anger or criticism. She felt like a shell of her former self, drained of all confidence and self-worth. She even began to question her own sanity.

Sarah's story is not unique. Millions of people find themselves trapped in relationships with narcissistic partners, unable to break free from the toxic cycle of abuse. Narcissism, a personality disorder characterized by an inflated sense of self-importance, a deep need for admiration, and a lack of empathy for others, is more prevalent than you might think. In fact, it is estimated that up to 5% of the population suffers from narcissistic personality disorder, and many more exhibit narcissistic traits.

In the labyrinthine dance of human relationships, few figures are as captivating and dangerous as the narcissist. With their seductive charm and magnetic presence, they lure us into a world of passion, intensity, and grand promises. Yet beneath this alluring facade lies a dark truth: a pervasive pattern of manipulation, exploitation, and emotional abuse that can leave even the most resilient individuals questioning their own self-worth, and sometimes even their sanity.

Narcissism is named after Narcissus, a tragic figure in ancient Greek mythology, who fell in love with his own image reflected in a pool of water and ultimately died of thirst because he would not disturb the water for fear of losing sight of his reflection. This cautionary tale is a powerful metaphor for the destructive nature of narcissistic relationships, where the narcissist's insatiable need for admiration and control can consume and destroy all those who they claim to love.

(Narcissus looking at his reflection)

Are you confused about your partner? Are they usually pleasant and sweet, but something seems "off" from time to time, and you can't put your finger on it? Do you question whether they are really in love with you or if they're merely saying nice things to get what THEY want? If these doubts resonate with you, read on.

Many of us tend to think that we could never find ourselves in a relationship with a narcissist. We tell ourselves, "That would never happen to me," or "I would know if my partner was a narcissist." But the truth is, **narcissists are masters of disguise, skilled in the art of presenting a false self to the world.** They can be charming, attentive, and seemingly devoted partners, all while harboring a profound lack of empathy and a ruthless drive to satisfy their own needs.

The *covert* narcissist, in particular, is a wolf in sheep's clothing, a master of deception who can infiltrate even the most guarded of hearts. With their subtle manipulation tactics and ability to mimic genuine human emotions, they can be exceptionally difficult to identify, leaving their victims trapped in a web of confusion, self-doubt, and emotional turmoil.

This book will shine a light into the dark corners of narcissistic relationships, empowering you with the knowledge and tools you need to identify, understand, and break free from the narcissist's toxic influence. As we share psychological insights, real-life examples, and practical strategies, we will guide you on a journey of self-discovery and liberation.

In Chapter 4, you will find a comprehensive self-assessment guide designed to help you evaluate your own relationship dynamics and determine whether you may be involved with a narcissist. This invaluable tool will provide you with the clarity and validation needed to trust your own perceptions and begin the process of reclaiming your autonomy and self-worth.

I understand the complexities of toxic relationships all too well. Growing up exposed to codependency, I found myself susceptible to narcissistic abuse and toxic relationships. After investing my energy, time, and sacrifice into two successive relationships that ultimately shattered, I decided to learn to interact, communicate, and love in a healthier way.

In my journey of re-education, I discovered that the first step to building better relationships is to love and be in sync with oneself. Armed with this knowledge, I not only transformed my own relationships and life but have also helped hundreds of people do the same.

My personal experiences have also made me acutely aware of the devastating impact that narcissistic abuse can have on an individual's mental health and well-being. Victims of narcissistic abuse often experience anxiety, depression, low self-esteem, and post-traumatic stress disorder (PTSD). They may feel isolated, confused, and trapped, unable to see a way out of their situation.

This has fueled my passion for helping others navigate the complex world of narcissistic relationships. By sharing my knowledge and experiences, I hope to empower readers with the tools they need to identify narcissistic behavior, recognize the red flags of abuse, and develop strategies for breaking free and healing.

Throughout this book, we will delve into the traits and behaviors of narcissists, the impact of narcissistic abuse on victims, and the steps you can take to reclaim your life and build healthier, more fulfilling relationships. Whether you are currently in a relationship with a narcissist, have recently left one, or simply want to avoid falling into the trap of narcissistic abuse, this book is for you.

By understanding the dynamics of narcissistic relationships and learning to prioritize your own well-being, you can break free from the cycle of abuse and create the life of authentic joy and connection that you truly deserve.

As you embark on this journey of self-discovery and healing, remember that you are not alone. Like Sarah, countless others have faced the same struggles and emerged stronger, wiser, and more resilient. With the right support, guidance, and determination, you too can break free from the grip of narcissistic abuse and build a happy and fulfilling future for yourself.

By arming yourself with knowledge and strategies, you can learn to identify, understand, and recover from manipulation, gaslighting, and other forms of narcissistic abuse. Let's get started!

Chapter 1: Understanding Narcissism

The charming mask

Julia met Tom at a friend's party. He was charismatic, intelligent, and incredibly attractive. Tom swept her off her feet with his grandiose gestures and lavish attention. He made her feel like the most special person in the world, and Julia quickly fell head over heels for him.

In the beginning, their relationship was a whirlwind romance. Tom showered Julia with expensive gifts, took her on spontaneous adventures, and constantly praised her beauty and intelligence. Julia felt like she had found her soulmate, someone who truly understood and appreciated her.

However, as the months passed, Julia began to notice subtle changes in Tom's behavior. He became increasingly critical of her, often making snide remarks about her appearance or belittling her accomplishments. When Julia expressed her hurt feelings, Tom would dismiss her and say she was being overly sensitive or had misunderstood.

Gradually, Tom's true colors started to show. He became more controlling, dictating who Julia could spend time with and how she should dress. He demanded constant attention and admiration, becoming angry and resentful when Julia failed to meet his demands. Just as Sarah had with David, Julia found herself walking on eggshells, constantly trying to anticipate Tom's moods and avoid triggering his temper.

What Julia experienced is a classic example of narcissistic behavior. Tom's initial charm and attentiveness were merely a mask, hiding his true nature. Narcissists often use a tactic called "love-bombing" to win over their partners, showering them with affection and attention in the early stages of the relationship. However, once they have secured their partner's devotion, the mask begins to slip, revealing their true, toxic nature.

Understanding narcissism is crucial for anyone who has found themselves trapped in a relationship with a narcissist. By recognizing the signs and patterns of narcissistic behavior, you can begin to make sense of your experiences and take steps to protect yourself from further abuse.

In the grand theatre of human existence, few characters captivate and unsettle us as deeply as the narcissist. With their grandiose sense of self-importance, their insatiable hunger for admiration, and their utter disregard for the feelings of others, narcissists leave an indelible mark on the lives they touch.

To truly understand the nature of narcissism, we must first peel back the layers of charm and charisma that often disguise the narcissist's true intentions. Like the sirens of ancient Greek mythology, whose enchanting songs lured unsuspecting sailors to their doom, narcissists possess a magnetic allure that can blind us to the dangerous undercurrents of their personality.

In this chapter, we will explore narcissism's traits, behaviors, and the impact it can have on relationships. We will examine the spectrum of narcissism, from mild to pathological, and discuss the common tactics used by narcissists to manipulate and control their victims.

By arming yourself with a clear understanding of narcissism, you can begin to unravel the confusion and chaos that often accompany narcissistic relationships. Let's begin and take the first step towards understanding this perplexing and often destructive personality disorder.

Narcissistic Personality Traits and Behaviors

Have you ever found yourself in a relationship where you felt constantly belittled, dismissed, or manipulated? Where your partner's needs always seemed to take precedence over your own, leaving you feeling drained and possibly even questioning your own reality? If so, you may have been the victim of a narcissist.

Narcissism is a personality disorder characterized by an inflated sense of self-importance, a deep need for admiration, and a lack of empathy for others. Narcissists often believe they are superior to others and have little regard for other people's feelings. They can be charming and captivating at first, but over time, their true colors begin to show.

You might recognize some of these common traits and behaviors:

1. Grandiosity: Narcissists have an exaggerated sense of self-importance, often believing they are uniquely special and deserving of admiration.

2. Entitlement: They expect special treatment and may disregard social norms or the needs of others in pursuit of their own desires.

3. Lack of empathy: Narcissists struggle to understand or acknowledge the feelings of others, often leaving their partners feeling unheard and invalidated.

4. Manipulation: They may use tactics like gaslighting, guilt-tripping, or love bombing to control and manipulate those around them.

5. Need for admiration: Narcissists crave constant attention and validation, often becoming angry or resentful when they don't receive it.

If you've experienced any of these behaviors in your relationship, know that you're not alone. Narcissistic abuse is far more common than many people realize, and it can leave deep emotional scars. But by understanding the nature of narcissism, you can begin to untangle yourself from its web and reclaim your sense of self.

Throughout history, narcissists have played pivotal roles in shaping the course of events, from the rise and fall of empires to the formation and structure of companies that impact the way we live to the way we perceive leaders and their influence on society. To understand the nature of narcissism, however, we must recognize the key traits and behaviors that define it.

At their core, narcissists are driven by an insatiable need for admiration and a grandiose sense of self-importance. They believe themselves to be superior to others, often viewing the world through a lens of entitlement and privilege. But this inflated sense of self is a fragile construct, requiring constant validation and praise from those around them.

In the words of the ancient Greek philosopher Aristotle, "The narcissist, being in love with himself, has no room for others." This lack of empathy is a hallmark of narcissistic behavior, enabling them to manipulate and exploit others without remorse. Like skilled puppeteers, they expertly pull the strings of those around them, using tactics like gaslighting, guilt-tripping, and love-bombing to maintain control and secure their own desires.

The Spectrum of Narcissism

Just as no two individuals are alike, narcissism manifests on a spectrum, ranging from mild traits to severe, pathological disorders.

In the realm of relationships, even milder forms of narcissism can cast a long shadow, eroding trust, intimacy, and emotional well-being. Like a slow poison, the narcissist's influence can seep into the very fabric of a partnership, leaving behind a trail of confusion, self-doubt, and pain.

Think of this spectrum like a scale, with healthy self-esteem on one end and pathological narcissism on the other. Someone with a few narcissistic traits might be self-centered or crave admiration but still maintain the ability to empathize with others. On the more severe end, those with narcissistic personality disorder (NPD) display a pervasive pattern of grandiosity, entitlement, and lack of empathy that significantly impairs their relationships and overall functioning.

Regardless of where your partner falls on this spectrum, if their narcissistic behaviors are causing you distress or harm, it's essential to prioritize your own well-being and take steps to protect yourself.

The Narcissist in Modern Society

A misunderstood label in the fast-paced, self-obsessed world of the 21st century, the term "narcissist" has become ubiquitous, carelessly thrown around in casual conversation and media headlines. From celebrities and politicians to coworkers and family members, it seems that everyone is quick to diagnose others with narcissism, often without a true understanding of this personality disorder.

As philosopher Jean Baudrillard observed, "We live in a world where there is more and more information, and less and less meaning." In the age of social media and instant gratification, the very concept of narcissism has been diluted, reduced to a mere caricature of its true psychological depth and significance.

The Rise of the "Narcissism Epidemic"

In recent years, there has been a growing concern among mental health professionals and social commentators about the apparent rise of narcissism in modern society. This phenomenon, often referred to as the "narcissism epidemic," suggests that our increasingly individualistic, self-focused culture is breeding a generation of entitled, self-absorbed individuals who prioritize their own needs and desires above all else.

One of the primary factors often cited in this supposed epidemic is the rise of social media and digital technology. Platforms like Facebook, Instagram, X and TikTok have created a virtual stage for individuals to present carefully curated versions of themselves to the world, often emphasizing their accomplishments, appearances, and social status. The instant gratification of likes, comments, and followers can create a powerful feedback loop, reinforcing narcissistic tendencies and encouraging users to prioritize their online image over their authentic selves.

Moreover, the anonymity and distance afforded by digital communication can sometimes embolden individuals to engage in more aggressive, confrontational, or self-aggrandizing behavior than they might in face-to-face interactions. The ability to hide behind a screen and project a false sense of superiority can be a breeding ground for narcissistic traits and behaviors.

However, it's important to approach the concept of the "narcissism epidemic" with a critical eye. While it's true that our modern culture places a high value on individualism, self-promotion, and personal branding, it's oversimplistic to suggest that this alone is causing a widespread increase in narcissistic personality disorder.

Narcissism, as a clinical diagnosis, is a complex and multifaceted condition that arises from a combination of genetic, environmental, and developmental factors. It cannot be reduced to a mere byproduct of social media or modern technology, nor can it be accurately diagnosed based on superficial observations of behavior or personality traits.

Furthermore, the tendency to casually label others as narcissists can itself be a form of narcissistic behavior, as it allows individuals to feel superior and dismissive of those they perceive as flawed or problematic. By reducing the complex reality of human behavior and relationships to a simple, one-dimensional label, we risk losing sight of the nuance, context, and depth that characterize true psychological understanding.

The Narcissist's Sense of Entitlement and Lack of Empathy

At the core of the narcissistic personality lies a toxic combination of entitlement and a profound lack of empathy. Narcissists believe themselves to be special, unique, and deserving of privileges and admiration beyond what is afforded to others. This grandiose self-image often leads them to believe they are above the law and exempt from the rules and responsibilities that govern the lives of the rest of us mortals.

As Bernie Madoff, infamous narcissist and convicted fraudster, once claimed, "In today's regulatory environment, it's virtually impossible to violate rules." This staggering lack of accountability and remorse is a hallmark of the narcissistic personality, as they go to great lengths to conceal their misdeeds and maintain their carefully crafted image of superiority.

One of the most chilling and defining characteristics of narcissists is their complete emotional disconnection from the feelings and experiences of others. This absence of empathy allows them to inflict pain and suffering on those around them without remorse, manipulating and exploiting others for their own gain.

In the words of psychologist and author Dr. Simon Baron-Cohen, "Empathy is the ability to imagine what someone else might be thinking or feeling, and to respond to their thoughts and feelings with an appropriate emotion." For narcissists, this fundamental human capacity is severely lacking, often replaced by a cold, calculating self-interest that knows no bounds.

While the Diagnostic and Statistical Manual of Mental Disorders (DSM) provides official guidelines for diagnosing narcissistic personality disorder, it is important to recognize the limitations of these criteria when it comes to identifying *covert* narcissists. These skilled manipulators are often able to mask their true nature during clinical evaluations, presenting a facade of normalcy and well-being that belies their underlying pathology.

The covert narcissist, with their deep-seated insecurities and hidden wounds, may be able to fool even the most experienced clinicians. This makes it all the more crucial for individuals to trust their own instincts and experiences when assessing the presence of narcissistic abuse in their lives, so they may protect themselves from further harm.

The Profound Selfishness of the Narcissist

At the core of the narcissistic personality lies a profound sense of selfishness: a complete disregard for the needs, feelings, and autonomy of others. This often manifests in the narcissist's propensity to shame and belittle those around them, using their sharp tongues and quick wits to inflict emotional wounds and assert their own superiority.

As philosopher and author Ayn Rand observed, "The narcissist has no self-esteem or self-respect. His only sense of self-worth comes from the image he projects to others." By tearing down those around them, the narcissist seeks to elevate their own fragile ego, feeding their insatiable need for admiration and control at the expense of the well-being of others.

The Narcissist's Resistance to Therapy: A Roadblock to Healing

One of the greatest challenges in addressing NPD is the narcissist's inherent resistance to therapy and self-reflection. Their grandiose self-image and deep-seated fear of vulnerability make it exceedingly difficult for them to acknowledge their own flaws and engage in the hard work of personal growth and change.

As psychologist and author Dr. Ramani Durvasula tells us, "Narcissists are notoriously difficult to treat in therapy because they don't believe there is anything wrong with them." This resistance to treatment poses a significant obstacle to healing, not only for the narcissist themselves but for the countless people whose lives have been impacted by their destructive behavior.

The Enigma of Narcissistic Abuse: Theories and Speculations

As we delve into the dark recesses of the narcissistic mind, a perplexing question arises: why do narcissists engage in such destructive and abusive behavior? Despite decades of research and countless theories, the underlying motivations behind narcissistic abuse remain shrouded in mystery.

Some experts speculate that narcissistic abuse stems from a deep-seated sense of insecurity and self-loathing, a desperate attempt to bolster a fragile ego by tearing down those around them. Others suggest that narcissists are driven by an insatiable hunger for power and control, a need to dominate and manipulate others in order to feel superior and invulnerable.

Yet, as Erich Fromm, renowned social psychologist and psychoanalyst, observed, "The narcissist is not self-loving, but self-hating to the core." Perhaps, in the end, the narcissist's abusive behavior is a tragic reflection of their own unresolved wounds and unmet needs, a misguided attempt to fill the gaping void within their own psyche.

The Narcissist's Modus Operandi: Using and Abusing Others

At the heart of the narcissist's interactions with others lies a pervasive pattern of exploitation and abuse, a relentless drive to use and manipulate those around them for their own selfish ends. Whether through charm, intimidation, or outright aggression, the narcissist views others as tools to be used and discarded at will, objects to be exploited for their own gratification and advantage.

Philosopher Immanuel Kant famously advised, "Always treat humanity, whether in yourself or in another, as an end in itself and never merely as a means." The narcissist, with their utter disregard for the autonomy and dignity of others, stands in direct opposition to this fundamental ethical principle, viewing the world and all those in it as nothing more than a means to their own twisted ends.

The Many Faces of Narcissism: Overt, Covert, Vulnerable, Grandiose, and Malignant

While the term "narcissist" is often used as a catch-all label, it is crucial to recognize that narcissism is not a monolithic entity, but as we have noted, a complex spectrum of traits and behaviors that can manifest in various forms and with varying degrees of severity. From the outwardly grandiose and attention-seeking overt narcissist to the more subtle and manipulative covert narcissist, the face of narcissism is as varied as it is troubling.

Other distinctions within the narcissistic spectrum include vulnerable narcissism, characterized by hypersensitivity to criticism and a tendency towards self-victimization, and malignant narcissism, a particularly dangerous and toxic form of narcissism that combines grandiosity, aggression, and paranoia.

The Covert Narcissist: The Ultimate Wolf in Sheep's Clothing

Among the various manifestations of narcissism, perhaps none is more insidious and challenging to identify than the covert narcissist. These master manipulators have perfected the art of disguise, presenting a facade of humility, sensitivity, and concern for others while hiding their true nature.

Like a wolf in sheep's clothing, the covert narcissist moves through the world undetected, silently preying on the vulnerabilities and good intentions of those around them. Their ability to mask their narcissistic traits and appear "normal" or even admirable makes them particularly difficult to spot and even harder to protect oneself against.

The covert narcissist adapts to the expectations and desires of those around them while secretly harboring a deep-seated need for admiration and control. This ability to hide in plain sight makes them particularly dangerous, as their victims may not even realize they are being manipulated until it is too late.

The Path Forward: Unmasking the Narcissist and Reclaiming Your Power

As we continue, remember that knowledge is power. By educating ourselves about the various faces and manifestations of narcissistic personality disorder, we begin to chip away at the narcissist's greatest weapon: their ability to deceive and manipulate.

In the following chapters, we will explore the specific patterns, tactics, and red flags associated with narcissistic abuse, with a particular focus on the challenges posed by the covert narcissist. Through a combination of expert insights, real-life examples, and practical strategies, we will work to unmask the narcissist, expose their true nature, and reclaim our own power and agency in the face of their toxic influence.

Shahida Arabi, poet and survivor of narcissistic abuse, reminds us, "The narcissist's greatest fear is that you will see them for who and what they really are: empty, pathetic, and worthless." When we shine a light on narcissism, we take the first step towards liberation and healing, toward a life free from the pain of narcissistic abuse and filled with genuine self-love, empathy, and connection.

Chapter 2:
Recognizing Narcissistic
Patterns in Relationships

Mark thought he had found the perfect partner in Olivia. She was beautiful, charming, and seemed to understand him like no one else ever had. In the beginning, their relationship was a whirlwind of passion and excitement. Olivia showered Mark with attention, compliments, and grand romantic gestures. She told him he was unlike anyone she had ever met before, and that they were destined to be together.

However, as the months passed, Mark began to notice subtle changes in Olivia's behavior. Her once-constant stream of affection became unpredictable. She would lavish him with praise one day, only to belittle him the next. She began to criticize his appearance, his career choices, and his friendships. "I'm only telling you this because I love you," she would say. "I want you to be the best version of yourself."

Mark was never sure what might trigger Olivia's disapproval or anger. She would accuse him of being too sensitive when he took offense at some of her remarks. "You're overreacting," she'd say dismissively. "Can't you take a joke?"

Olivia's controlling behavior extended to all aspects of Mark's life. She insisted on knowing his whereabouts at all times and would become annoyed if he didn't respond to her texts immediately. She discouraged him from spending time with his friends and family, claiming that they were a bad influence on him. "Why do you need them when you have me?" she would ask.

When Mark pushed back or expressed his own needs, Olivia would accuse him of being selfish. She would tell him how lucky he was to have her in his life and insist thet he would be nothing without her. "No one else would put up with you like I do," she'd say, leaving Mark feeling guilty for wanting something else.

Despite the emotional turmoil, Mark struggled to leave the relationship. He had invested so much of himself into making things work with Olivia, and he hated the thought of being alone. He also felt a deep sense of responsibility for her happiness, believing that if he could just be a better partner, things would improve.

As Mark sat in his car after another draining argument with Olivia, he found himself questioning his own perceptions. Was he really as flawed and unworthy as she made him feel? Or was there something more sinister at play in their relationship?

Mark's story illustrates the complex and often confusing nature of narcissistic relationships. Like many victims of narcissistic abuse, Mark struggled to recognize the signs of manipulation and emotional abuse, even as they took a toll on his self-esteem and well-being.

The truth is, narcissistic abuse can be insidious, gradually eroding your sense of self. Narcissists, especially those of the covert variety, are skilled at masking their true nature, presenting a facade of charm, empathy, and vulnerability to the outside world (Ettensohn, 2016). It's this very ability to blend in and appear "normal" that makes recognizing narcissistic patterns in relationships so challenging.

So, how can you tell if your partner's behavior is a sign of narcissistic abuse, or simply a normal, albeit frustrating, part of any long-term relationship? In this chapter, we'll explore the common patterns and red flags of narcissistic relationships, helping you to identify the warning signs so you can take action to change your circumstances.

The Idealization Phase: Love Bombing and the Narcissistic Honeymoon

In the early stages of a relationship with a narcissist, you may feel like you've found your perfect match. Narcissists often engage in a tactic known as "love bombing," showering their new partner with excessive affection, attention, and grand gestures of devotion (Brame, 2015). This intense idealization phase can be intoxicating, leaving you feeling swept off your feet and convinced that you've found your soulmate.

However, this 'honeymoon' phase is rarely built on a foundation of genuine love and connection. Instead, it serves as a means for the narcissist to quickly forge a bond with you, creating a sense of intimacy and trust that they can later exploit for their own gain (Campbell & Foster, 2002). By making you feel special, understood, and valued, the narcissist lays the groundwork for future manipulation and control.

The Devaluation Phase: Criticism, Gaslighting, and Emotional Abuse

As the novelty of the idealization phase wears off, narcissists often transition into a period of devaluation, characterized by increasing criticism, belittlement, and emotional abuse. This shift can be jarring and confusing, as the once adoring partner you fell in love with seems to transform before your eyes.

Narcissists may begin to criticize your appearance, undermine your accomplishments, or compare you unfavorably to others. They may engage in gaslighting, a form of psychological manipulation in which they deny or distort what you believe, causing you to question your own perceptions and memories (Stern, 2018). Over time, this constant erosion of your self-esteem can leave you feeling anxious, depressed, and unsure of yourself.

The Discard Phase: Abandonment and the Cycle of Abuse

In the final stage of the narcissistic cycle, the discard phase, a narcissist may abruptly end the relationship, often with little or no explanation. This abandonment can be devastating, leaving you feeling worthless, and struggling to make sense of what went wrong.

It's important to recognize, though, that this discard phase is rarely the end of the story. Narcissists often engage in a cyclical pattern, returning to their former partners with promises of change and a renewed sense of idealization (Louis de Canonville, 2015). This tactic can be incredibly difficult to resist, as the narcissist plays on your deepest desires for love and validation, drawing you back into the toxic cycle once again.

Red Flags in Relationships: Spotting the Warning Signs of Narcissistic Abuse

Love Bombing: The Narcissist's Secret Weapon

Love bombing refers to when a narcissist showers their target with excessive affection, attention, and grand gestures of devotion, often to the point of seeming too good to be true (Brame, 2015). While it's normal to feel excited and swept off your feet in the beginning of a new relationship, love bombing takes this to an extreme level. Narcissists may bombard you with constant text messages, lavish gifts, and declarations of love in order to create a sense of intimacy and trust.

Dr. Ramani Durvasula notes, "Love bombing is a manipulative tactic designed to create a sense of intensity and dependency in the relationship. It's not about genuine love or connection, but rather about control and power" (Durvasula, 2018).

In other words, this phase is a calculated move, designed to disarm and secure the devotion of their target. Once they have established a hold over their partner, they begin to employ more insidious tactics, like gaslighting.

Gaslighting and Manipulation: Eroding Your Sense of Reality

Gaslighting can take many forms, from denying events that you know took place, to twisting your words and using them against you. Narcissists may also engage in blame-shifting, making you feel responsible for their own hurtful behavior or emotional outbursts.

Over time, these tactics can leave you feeling confused, anxious, and unsure of yourself. You may begin to question your own judgment and even memory as the narcissist's distorted version of reality takes hold.

As 16th-century Florentine philosopher Niccolò Machiavelli wrote in *The Prince*, "Men are so simple and so much inclined to obey immediate needs that a deceiver will never lack victims for his deceptions." The narcissist, skilled in the art of deception, knows precisely how to exploit the vulnerabilities of their partners, keeping them trapped in a cycle of confusion, self-doubt, and emotional turmoil.

Boundary Violations: Disregarding Your Needs and Autonomy

Narcissists have little regard for the personal boundaries and autonomy of others, often viewing their partners as extensions of themselves rather than separate individuals with their own needs and desires. This can manifest in a variety of boundary-violating behaviors, such as:

1. Invading your privacy by reading your text messages or emails

2. Disregarding your need for alone time or space

3. Making important decisions without consulting you

4. Pressuring you to engage in activities or behaviors that make you uncomfortable

Emotional Unavailability: The Narcissist's Empty Promises

Despite their grand gestures and declarations of love, narcissists are often emotionally unavailable to their partners. They may struggle to empathize with your feelings, dismiss your concerns, or simply tune out when you express your needs or desires.

This emotional unavailability can be particularly confusing and painful, as their words often don't align with their actions. They may promise you the world in one moment, only to withdraw or become cold and distant the next.

In his book, *Rethinking Narcissism,* Dr. Craig Malkin explains, "Narcissists can be very good at faking empathy and making empty promises. But when it comes to actually showing up and being there for their partners in a genuine way, they often fall short" (Malkin, 2015).

Controlling Behavior: The Narcissist's Need for Dominance

Narcissists have an insatiable need for control and dominance in their relationships, often going to great lengths to ensure that their partners are compliant and submissive. This behavior can take many forms, such as:

1. Dictating how you dress or wear your hair

2. Monitoring your whereabouts or social interactions

3. Controlling your access to money or resources

4. Isolating you from friends and family

As Dr. Durvasula notes, "Narcissists need to feel in control at all times. They may use a variety of tactics, from subtle manipulation to overt aggression, to maintain that sense of power and dominance in the relationship" (Durvasula, 2018).

To arm oneself against the narcissist's machinations, it is critical to be able to recognize these red flags. From the charming facade that masks a lack of empathy to the constant need for admiration and control, the signs are there for those who know where to look.

Some additional signs to watch out for include a charming, charismatic persona that seems too good to be true, a sense of entitlement or superiority, and a lack of empathy for others' feelings. Narcissists may also have a history of blaming others, lying, or exaggerating, and they often move quickly in relationships, seeking intimacy and commitment before you've had a chance to really get to know them. Other common tactics include guilt-tripping, isolating you from friends and family, and intermittent reinforcement – alternating between loving and dismissive behavior to keep you off-balance and seeking their approval.

If you've ever experienced any of the following, try to see them for what they are: tactics designed to maintain control and fulfill the narcissist's own needs:

- A whirlwind romance that seems too good to be true

- A partner who has a constant need for admiration and validation

- A partner who seems to lack empathy or concern for your feelings

- Cycles of idealization, devaluation, and discarding

- A partner who is unable to take responsibility or apologize for hurtful behavior

Healthy Love vs. Narcissistic Manipulation

It's crucial to differentiate between the nurturing, supportive dynamics of a healthy relationship and the toxic, manipulative patterns of a bond with a narcissist. By understanding the traits and behaviors that distinguish true love from narcissistic control, you can gain clarity on your own relationship and do what is necessary for your future emotional well-being.

Reflecting on Your Partner's Behavior: Distinguishing Love from Manipulation

One of the most challenging aspects of being in a relationship with a narcissist is the constant confusion between what feels like love and what is actually manipulation. Narcissists are skilled at creating an illusion of intimacy and connection, but these displays of affection are rarely genuine, serving instead as a means to secure loyalty and maintain control (Durvasula, 2019).

To distinguish between true love and narcissistic manipulation, you must look beyond surface-level gestures and examine the deeper patterns of behavior in your relationship. Dr. Durvasula explains, "Narcissists may say all the right things, but their actions rarely match their words. True love is consistent, reliable, and respectful, while narcissistic manipulation is erratic, self-serving, and often cruel" (Durvasula, 2019, p. 75).

Traits of a Narcissistic Partner

Narcissistic partners exhibit a range of destructive behaviors that can erode your sense of self and leave you feeling trapped and powerless. Some common behaviors of narcissists include:

1. Refusal to take responsibility for their actions or mistakes

2. Projection of their own abusive behavior onto others

3. Hypersensitivity to criticism or perceived slights

4. Pitting people against one another to maintain control

5. Betrayal and bullying tactics to keep you in line

6. Grandiose assertions of superiority and omnipotence

7. Indifference, impatience, or anger towards your needs and feelings

8. Coercion and pressure to conform to their demands

9. Attempts to isolate you from friends and family in order to maintain their control

10. An erosion of your free will and attempts to instill a sense of powerlessness

11. Punishment and retaliation for perceived disobedience

Traits of a Loving Partner

In contrast to the toxic dynamics of a narcissistic relationship, a healthy, loving partnership is characterized by mutual respect, empathy, and support. Some key behaviors of a loving partner include:

1. Respect for your thoughts, feelings, and boundaries

2. Standing up for you and defending you to others

3. Believing in you and your abilities

4. Listening to you and valuing your perspective

5. Genuinely wanting you to be happy and fulfilled

6. Cherishing your body and prioritizing your pleasure

7. Valuing you as an important part of their life

8. Supporting your adventures and personal growth

9. Celebrating your achievements and being empathetic with your struggles

10. Prioritizing your well-being

11. Honesty that comes from a place of love and respect

12. Trusting and respecting your instincts and decisions

13. Encouraging you to pursue your dreams and passions

14. Demonstrating their love through consistent actions, not just words

Signs You May Be in a Relationship with a Narcissist

If you find yourself constantly questioning the health and stability of your relationship, you may be involved with a narcissist. Some red flags to watch out for include:

1. Fearing disagreement or confrontation due to potential retaliation

2. Being told that you have problematic traits that no one else has mentioned

3. Struggling to have enjoyable, lighthearted conversations with them

4. Doubting their intentions and questioning their behavior

5. Noticing that they make subtle, critical comments about you

6. Being accused of lying, cheating, or other behaviors that they themselves engage in

7. Believing that nothing you do is ever good enough for your partner

8. Feeling provoked, picked on, or subtly undermined

9. Feeling embarrassed or ashamed about how they treat you, and hiding details from others

10. Compromising your morals and values to keep your partner happy

11. Feeling frustrated by your inability to convey the problematic nature of their behavior

12. Doubting your own perceptions and understanding of events

13. Realizing that you don't experience this dynamic with others

14. Feeling unsure about whether your partner is wonderful or terrible

15. Worrying that the relationship issues are your fault or that you've sabotaged things

16. Living in a state of constant confusion and uncertainty about your relationship

If you recognize these signs in your relationship, it's important to trust your instincts and seek support from friends, family, or mental health professionals. Remember, you are not alone, and there is hope for healing and reclaiming your life after narcissistic abuse.

Narcissistic Relationship Dynamics: The Insidious Nature of Manipulation

As we continue to explore the complexities of narcissistic relationships, it becomes increasingly clear that manipulation is the cornerstone of the narcissist's toolkit. Like a skilled puppeteer, they pull the strings of their partner's emotions, keeping them off-balance and under their control. In this section, we'll explore the various signs of manipulation that often characterize narcissistic relationship dynamics.

One of the most common manipulation tactics employed by narcissists is the use of implicit threats to ensure their partner's compliance. They may subtly suggest that if you don't do as they wish, they will make your life difficult or even unbearable (Stern, 2018). This could manifest as threats to withhold affection, financial support, or even access to your own children.

As Robert Greene observes in his book, *The 48 Laws of Power*, "The threat of violence or the hint of trouble can be more powerful than actual violence or trouble. It is the threat that controls, not the violence itself" (Greene, 1998, p. 231). The narcissist understands this principle all too well, using the specter of negative consequences to keep their victim in line and maintain their grip on the relationship.

The Insatiable Narcissist: Pushing for More, No Matter the Cost

Narcissists are notorious for their insatiable appetite for attention, admiration, and control. No matter how much you give of yourself, it never seems to be enough to satisfy their endless demands (Hotchkiss, 2003). They will push for more and more, disregarding your own needs, wants, and boundaries in the process.

This relentless pursuit of their own gratification is a hallmark of the narcissistic personality, as they view their partners not as autonomous individuals, but as mere extensions of themselves. Immanuel Kant argued, "A person must never be treated merely as a means to an end, but always at the same time as an end in themselves" (Kant, 1785/1998, p. 41). The narcissist, however, routinely violates this fundamental principle, using their partner as a tool to achieve their own selfish aims.

The Narcissist's Toolbox: Money, Fear, Love, Guilt, and Sex

To maintain control over their partners, narcissists leverage various tools. They may withhold financial support or they may even lavish gifts on you to keep you dependent on their generosity (Durvasula, 2019). They may exploit your fears and insecurities, using them to erode your self-esteem and keep you in a state of constant anxiety.

Narcissists may also weaponize love and affection, showering you with attention one moment and withdrawing it the next, leaving you desperate for their approval (Malkin, 2015). They may use guilt as a means of manipulation, making you feel responsible for their happiness or misery, and pressuring you to prioritize their needs above your own.

In intimate relationships, narcissists may use sex as a tool of control, either withholding physical affection to punish you or using sexual prowess to keep you ensnared (Schneider & Corley, 2002). They may make promises of future commitment or devotion, contingent upon your compliance with their demands, only to renege on these promises once they have gotten what they want from you.

The Narcissist's Bizarre Tales: A Case Study in Gaslighting

One of the strangest and most disorienting aspects of being in a relationship with a narcissist is their propensity for telling outlandish, fabricated stories that may be bizarre and far-fetched. These tales often serve to manipulate, control, and gaslight their victims, creating a distorted reality that keeps the victim off-balance and dependent on the narcissist.

An extreme real-life example of this phenomenon is the case of John Meehan, better known as "Dirty John." This story, which gained national attention through a popular podcast and TV series, illustrates the lengths to which some narcissists are willing to go to create and maintain their fabricated realities.

Debra Newell, a successful interior designer, met John Meehan through an online dating site. He was charming and presented himself as a successful anesthesiologist who had just returned from a year with Doctors Without Borders. In reality, Meehan was a former nurse anesthetist with a history of drug abuse, criminal behavior, and manipulating women.

Throughout their two-month romance and then marriage, Meehan spun increasingly elaborate lies to maintain his façade and isolate Debra from her family. He claimed to have attended prestigious universities, fabricated stories about his past heroics, and even wore surgical scrubs around the house to maintain the illusion of his medical career.

When Debra's family became suspicious and tried to warn her, Meehan intensified his gaslighting efforts. He convinced Debra that her family was jealous and trying to sabotage their relationship. He manipulated her into believing that she couldn't trust her own perceptions or the concerns of those who cared about her.

The "Dirty John" case demonstrates how narcissists can create entire false personas and maintain them through a combination of charm, manipulation, and gaslighting. It also highlights the devastating impact these lies can have on their victims and their families.

While admittedly this is an over-the-top example, it nevertheless serves as a stark reminder of the importance of trusting one's instincts and maintaining connections with supportive friends and family who can provide reality checks when needed. It also underscores the need for vigilance in recognizing the red flags of narcissistic behavior, even when they're disguised behind a charming façade.

As poet Maya Angelou so eloquently stated, "You may not control all the events that happen to you, but you can decide not to be reduced by them" (Angelou, 2009, p. 267). In the face of narcissistic manipulation, hold fast to your own truth, your own worth, and your own resilience. With time, patience, and self-compassion, you can emerge from the darkness of narcissistic abuse and step into the light of a brighter, healthier future.

Chapter 3:
The Impact of Narcissism on Partners

Michael had always prided himself on his strength of character and self-confidence. A successful software engineer, he never imagined he'd find himself trapped in a relationship that left him feeling powerless and miserable. But that was before he met Sophia.

When they first started dating, Sophia seemed like a dream come true. She was beautiful, charismatic, and seemed to connect with Michael on a deep level. She always made him feel like the most important person in the world.

As the months passed, however, Michael began to notice a darker side to Sophia's personality. Her mood would shift suddenly and dramatically, leaving him constantly on edge. She became increasingly critical of various aspects of his life when he wasn't with her, such as his job, and his friends and family. "Don't you want to be the best version of yourself for me?" she would ask.

As her negative critiques escalated, Michael found himself withdrawing from his friends and family. He stopped going to the gym, an activity he had once loved, because Sophia accused him of flirting with other women there. He began to doubt his own perceptions and memories, as Sophia would often deny events that he clearly remembered or insist that he had said or done things he knew he hadn't.

The constant emotional turmoil began to take a toll on Michael's physical health as well. He developed bouts of insomnia, often lying awake at night replaying arguments in his head and trying to figure out how to avoid setting Sophia off the next day. He had chronic headaches and digestive issues, which his doctor attributed to stress.

In spite of all this, Michael was hesitant to leave. He had tried hard to make things work with Sophia, and he hated the idea of admitting defeat. He wondered how he, a successful and intelligent man, had allowed himself to become so diminished by someone who claimed to love him.

It wasn't until a concerned coworker gently pointed out the changes in Michael's behavior and demeanor that he began to realize the extent of the abuse he had been enduring. He started to research narcissistic abuse and was shocked to find how closely his experiences aligned with the patterns he read about.

Michael's story is another example of the far-reaching impact that narcissistic abuse can have on its victims, regardless of gender or background. The emotional, psychological, and even physical toll of such relationships can be highly destructive, leaving deep scars that take time and effort to heal.

Countless individuals find themselves trapped in the toxic web of narcissistic abuse, suffering emotional and psychological wounds that can take years to heal. In this chapter, we'll explore the profound impact of narcissistic abuse on the partners of narcissists, shedding light on the insidious ways in which this form of emotional manipulation can erode one's sense of self-worth and sometimes even one's perception of reality.

The Emotional and Psychological Toll of Narcissistic Abuse

Narcissistic abuse is a form of emotional and psychological manipulation that can have devastating effects on the mental health and well-being of the narcissist's partner. While physical scars of abuse may be visible to the outside world, the emotional and psychological wounds inflicted by a narcissist often remain hidden, leaving the victim feeling isolated and alone.

One of the most common emotional effects of narcissistic abuse is anxiety and depression (Bonchay, 2018). The constant stress of walking on eggshells, never knowing when the narcissist will lash out or withdraw their affection, can take a tremendous toll on the victim's mental health. They may experience panic attacks, insomnia, or a pervasive sense of dread, constantly bracing themselves for the next emotional onslaught.

In addition to anxiety and depression, narcissistic abuse often leads to a profound erosion of one's self-esteem and sense of self-worth (Hotchkiss, 2003). The constant criticism, belittling, and gaslighting can cause one to doubt their own abilities, intelligence, and even their fundamental value as a human being. They may feel like a mere shell of their former selves, having lost touch with the confident, self-assured person they once were.

The cognitive dissonance created by the narcissist's hot-and-cold behavior can also be profoundly disorienting for their partner (Malkin, 2015). One moment, the narcissist may be showering them with love and affection, and the next, they may be raging at them over a perceived slight. This unpredictability can leave the victim feeling constantly on edge, never knowing which version of their partner they will encounter from one day to the next.

Over time, the trauma of narcissistic abuse can lead to a phenomenon known as trauma bonding (Carnes, 2019). This is a psychological response in which the victim becomes emotionally attached to their abuser, often feeling a perverse sense of loyalty or even love towards them. Trauma bonding can make it incredibly difficult for the victim to leave the abusive relationship, as they may feel like they are betraying their partner or giving up on the relationship.

The Cognitive Dissonance of Narcissistic Abuse

One of the most perplexing and distressing aspects of being in a relationship with a narcissist is the experience of cognitive dissonance - the mental and emotional strain of holding two conflicting beliefs or perceptions at the same time.

For victims, this often manifests as a split in their memories and feelings towards the narcissist. On one hand, they may have cherished memories of the good times in the relationship, the moments of tenderness, passion, and connection that initially drew them to their partner. These memories can be so powerful and compelling that they find themselves defending the narcissist when others express concerns or criticisms about their behavior.

On the other hand, the victim may also have a wealth of painful, traumatic memories of the narcissist's abusive behavior. These memories can be so raw and overwhelming that they begin wondering how they could have ever believed in the narcissist's facade of love and care.

The push and pull between these two sets of memories can be disorienting. The victim may feel like they are constantly at war with themselves, torn between their longing for the idealized version of the relationship and the undeniable reality of the abuse they have suffered.

This internal conflict is a hallmark of cognitive dissonance, and it is a common experience among survivors of narcissistic abuse. The narcissist's ability to present a charming, charismatic persona alongside their abusive behavior creates a mental and emotional trap that can be incredibly difficult to break free from.

The Insidious Nature of Trauma Bonding

As mentioned above, trauma bonding occurs when the victim develops a strong emotional attachment to their abuser, often feeling a sense of loyalty or love toward the person who is causing them harm (Carnes, 2019). At first glance, this may seem counterintuitive, as many wonder why anyone would feel a positive connection to someone who belittles, manipulates, and abuses them. But narcissistic relationships involve complex psychological dynamics.

Narcissists are skilled at intermittently reinforcing their partner's affection and dependence, interspersing moments of tenderness and charm amidst the abuse (Bonchay, 2018). This inconsistent behavior creates a powerful cycle of hope and disappointment, keeping the victim emotionally invested in the relationship and convinced that the narcissist's "true self" is the loving, attentive partner they occasionally see.

An Example of Trauma Bonding

Consider the story of Rachel and David. When Rachel first met David, she was swept off her feet by all the usual characteristics we've already described in a narcissist. Of course, as the relationship progressed, David became increasingly controlling and possessive, demanding that Rachel constantly check in with him and accusing her of flirting with other men. Just as we have described in previous examples of these types of relationships, he criticized her appearance, belittled or dismissed her accomplishments, and flew into rages over perceived slights.

Despite this behavior, Rachel found herself deeply attached to David. When he showed her affection or apologized for his outbursts, she felt a rush of relief and gratitude, convincing herself that his cruelty was an aberration and that the "real" David was the loving, attentive man she had fallen for.

Even when her friends and family began expressing concern about David's behavior, she fiercely defended him, feeling a sense of loyalty and protectiveness toward him. It took years of escalating abuse and a crisis point in the relationship for Rachel to finally recognize the trauma bond for what it was and to seek help to free herself.

The Physical and Social Toll of Narcissistic Abuse

In addition to the profound emotional and psychological effects of narcissistic abuse, victims often experience a range of physical and social consequences that can have a lasting impact on their health and well-being.

Isolation from Friends and Family

One of the hallmarks of narcissistic relationships is the gradual isolation of the victim from their support networks (Louis de Canonville, 2015). Narcissists often see their partner's friends and family as threats to their control, and may actively work to distance the victim from these relationships.

They may criticize the victim's loved ones, making disparaging comments about their character or motives. They may also monopolize the victim's time and attention, leaving little room for outside relationships. Over time, the victim may find themselves increasingly cut off from the people who once provided them with love, support, and a sense of perspective.

Physical Health Issues Due to Stress

The chronic stress of living with a narcissist can take a serious toll on the victim's physical health (Durvasula, 2019). They may experience a range of stress-related symptoms, such as headaches, digestive problems, and chronic fatigue. The constant state of hypervigilance and fear can also lead to sleep disturbances, weakening the immune system and leaving the victim more vulnerable to illness.

In addition, the shame and self-doubt instilled by the narcissist may cause the victim to neglect their own self-care, foregoing exercise, healthy eating, and regular medical check-ups. Over time, these physical health issues can compound, exacerbating one's overall sense of helplessness and despair, and taking a toll on the body, leading to a range of health issues and complications.

Some common physical symptoms reported by survivors of narcissistic abuse include:

- Weight gain or weight loss

- Chronic fatigue and exhaustion

- Digestive problems and gastrointestinal distress

- Headaches and migraines

- Insomnia or other sleep disturbances

- Weakened immune system and increased susceptibility to illness

Listening to Your Body's Wisdom

One of the most important things to remember when it comes to narcissistic abuse is to trust your own instincts and listen to your body's signals. Often, our bodies are aware of the danger and toxicity of a situation long before our conscious minds are willing to acknowledge it (Northrup, 2018).

You may find yourself feeling constantly on edge, jumpy, or nauseated when in your partner's presence. You may experience a sense of dread or heaviness when anticipating interactions with them. Your gut may be telling you that something is profoundly wrong, even if you can't quite put your finger on what it is.

These signals are your body's way of sounding the alarm, urging you to pay attention and take action to protect yourself. You must honor these signals, even if the narcissist is working hard to convince you that you're being irrational or oversensitive.

Sex with a Narcissist: The Intimate Battlefield

In the world of narcissistic relationships, the bedroom can become a microcosm of the larger power dynamics at play. For many partners of narcissists, sex becomes yet another arena in which their needs, desires, and autonomy are subordinated to those of their partner.

The Tell-Tale Signs:

One of the most striking red flags of a narcissistic sexual partner is their pervasive self-centeredness in the bedroom. They may view sex not as a mutually enjoyable experience, but rather as a means to fulfill their own needs and assert their dominance over their partner (Streep, 2016).

Narcissists may be excessively focused on their own pleasure, paying little attention to their partner's desires or satisfaction. They may pressure their partner to engage in sexual acts that make them uncomfortable, or may be dismissive or even mocking of their partner's sexual needs and preferences.

This self-centeredness can manifest in a variety of ways. They may insist on sexual positions or activities that prioritize their own gratification, while disregarding their partner's comfort or enjoyment. They may be unwilling to engage in foreplay or may rush through it impatiently, seeing it as an unnecessary obstacle to their own satisfaction.

Narcissists may also be critical of their partner's sexual performance, making disparaging comments about their body, their techniques, or their responsiveness. This criticism can be deeply wounding, eroding their partner's self-esteem and making them feel inadequate or undesirable.

The Taboo Topic: Difficulty Discussing with Others

For many victims of narcissistic abuse, the topic of sex can be particularly challenging to discuss with friends or family members. The deep sense of shame, self-doubt, and confusion that often accompanies narcissistic abuse can make it difficult for victims to open up about their experiences, even to trusted confidants.

Moreover, the intimate nature of sex can make it feel especially taboo or embarrassing to share with others. Victims may fear being judged, blamed, or misunderstood, further compounding their sense of isolation and despair.

This difficulty in discussing sexual issues can be particularly pronounced in cases where the narcissist has engaged in more overt forms of sexual coercion or violence. Victims may feel a deep sense of humiliation or self-blame, believing that they somehow brought the abuse upon themselves or should have been able to prevent it.

But the shame and secrecy surrounding sexual abuse are tools that narcissists use to maintain their power and control. By breaking the silence and reaching out for support, victims can begin to challenge the narcissist's narrative and reclaim their own voice and agency.

The Honeymoon Phase:

During the 'honeymoon phase,' a narcissist may go out of their way to fulfill their partner's every sexual fantasy, making them feel cherished, desired, and deeply connected. They may spend hours exploring their partner's body, whispering sweet nothings, and promising a lifetime of passion and devotion.

But this period of idealization is often short-lived, giving way to a more self-centered and manipulative dynamic as the relationship progresses. Once the narcissist feels secure in their partner's attachment and dependence, they may begin to withdraw their affection and attention, using sex as a tool for reward and punishment.

Victims may find themselves constantly striving to recapture the magic of the honeymoon phase, going to great lengths to please and appease their narcissistic partner in the hopes of earning back their love and desire. This cycle of idealization and devaluation can be exhausting and demoralizing, leaving victims feeling like they are chasing an impossible dream.

The Insidious Effects: Feelings of Being Used and Inability to Orgasm

As the narcissistic relationship takes hold, many partners begin to experience a pervasive sense of being used or objectified in the bedroom. They may feel like their body is merely a tool for their partner's gratification, rather than a source of mutual pleasure and connection.

This objectification can have a profound impact on the victim's ability to enjoy sexual intimacy. They may find it difficult or even impossible to achieve orgasm, as the stress, anxiety, and emotional disconnection of the relationship take their toll on their sexual response (Durvasula, 2019).

The narcissist's self-centered approach to sex can also leave their partner feeling emotionally unfulfilled. Without the sense of mutual care, respect, and attunement that characterizes healthy sexual intimacy, the victim may feel increasingly alienated from their own body and desires.

Over time, this disconnection can lead to a host of sexual difficulties, including low libido, painful intercourse, and an aversion to sexual touch. These issues can be further compounded by the narcissist's lack of empathy or concern, as they may see their partner's struggles as a personal affront or a sign of their own inadequacy.

The Intuitive Alarm: Trusting Your Gut

Despite the narcissist's efforts to gaslight and manipulate their partner, many partners of narcissists report a persistent, intuitive sense that something is amiss in the relationship. This gut feeling may be particularly pronounced in the realm of sexual intimacy, where the narcissist's self-centeredness and lack of empathy can be evident.

Victims may find themselves wondering if they are being overly sensitive or unreasonable in their expectations of mutual care and respect. They may second-guess their own sexual responses, blaming themselves for their inability to feel aroused or satisfied. This intuitive alarm is often a sign that their needs and boundaries are being violated, and that the narcissist's behavior is fundamentally unhealthy and abusive.

It's essential to learn to trust your own instincts and listen to the quiet voice within that tells you something is wrong. By learning to tune into your own inner wisdom and trusting the signals your body is sending you, you can begin to reclaim your own sexual agency and autonomy.

The Blame Game: Recognizing the Narcissist's Role

Many of those on the receiving end of a narcissist's tactics tend to internalize blame and responsibility for the problems in the relationship. This is particularly true when it comes to sexual intimacy, where victims may feel like their own desires and responses are flawed.

As we've learned, narcissists are highly skilled at shifting blame and responsibility onto their partners, making them feel like they are the ones who are defective or problematic. They may tell their partner that their sexual needs are excessive or unreasonable, that their desires are perverted or shameful, or that their difficulties with arousal or orgasm are a sign of their own inadequacy.

Over time, this constant barrage of criticism and blame can erode one's self-esteem and sense of sexual worth. If you're in a relationship with a narcissist who's engaging in this type of abuse, it's important to recognize that difficulties with sexual intimacy are not a reflection of your worth or desirability, but rather a product of your partner's toxic behavior. By placing the blame where it belongs, you can move down the path toward healing and improve self-esteem.

This can be a challenging process, as your partner's voice may have become deeply internalized over the course of your relationship. Consider working with a therapist or support group to cope with the feelings of blame and shame that have accompanied the sexual experience over the course of your relationship.

Learning to recognize the narcissist's role in creating the sexual difficulties within your relationship is the first step toward seeing yourself as whole, desirable, and worthy of love and respect, both in and out of the bedroom.

The Long Con: Love Bombing and Intermittent Reinforcement

The insidious nature of love bombing and intermittent reinforcement can make it difficult to recognize narcissistic sexual abuse. Even as the overall relationship becomes increasingly toxic, the narcissist may continue to intersperse moments of seeming tenderness, passion, and intimacy amidst the manipulation (Bonchay, 2018), and this can be confusing.

These fleeting glimpses of the person you fell for can create a powerful sense of cognitive dissonance, making it difficult to reconcile their bad behavior with the loving facade they occasionally present. As a victim, you may cling to these moments of connection, hoping they represent the "real" person beneath the abusive behavior.

The narcissist may even use these moments of affection and passion as a tool of intermittent reinforcement, keeping their victim hooked and invested in the relationship. Just as a slot machine keeps gamblers coming back for more with the promise of an occasional payout, the narcissist's sporadic displays of love and desire can keep their victim hoping for a return to the bliss of the honeymoon phase.

This cycle of idealization and devaluation can be very difficult to escape, as you become conditioned to associate the narcissist with the highest highs and the lowest lows. You may start to feel a kind of addiction to your partner's love and approval, even though you recognize the destructive impact the relationship is having on your psyche.

By learning to see that the moments of tenderness and passion are not genuine expressions of love or care, but rather tools of manipulation and control, you can begin to move toward freedom from the toxicity of narcissism and focus on your own well-being.

The Ultimate Betrayal: When Sex No Longer Feels Good

For many partners of narcissists, there comes a point when sex is no longer feels pleasurable, safe, or emotionally connected. The pervasive sense of being used, objectified, and disregarded can take a profound toll, leading to feelings of numbness, dissociation, or even revulsion (Northrup, 2018).

This loss of sexual intimacy and pleasure can be one of the most painful and disorienting aspects of narcissistic abuse, as it strikes at the very heart of the romantic partnership. Victims may feel like they have lost a fundamental part of themselves, as their sexuality becomes tainted by their partner's manipulation. Difficulty with sexual intimacy may become yet another source of shame and self-recrimination, as they blame themselves for their inability to enjoy or desire their partner. They may feel like they are broken or defective, further compounding the emotional and psychological toll of being in a relationship with a narcissist.

It's important to recognize that this disconnect is not a reflection of your own desirability or sexual worth, but a product of your partner's inability to engage in mutual and empathetic intimacy.

As you educate yourself about narcissistic abuse and work toward healing, reclaiming a sense of sexual agency and pleasure can be a powerful step in the journey towards wholeness and self-love. This may involve working with a sex therapist or counselor to process the trauma and reestablish a healthy relationship with your body and desires.

It may also involve setting clear boundaries around sexual intimacy, both with the narcissist (if you remain in the relationship) and with future partners. By learning to prioritize your own needs, desires, and comfort, you can reclaim the feelings of joy, connection, and empowerment that surround a healthy sexuality.

Ultimately, there is no one-size-fits-all approach, and what works for one person may not work for another. But by seeking support, educating yourself, and learning to trust your instincts and boundaries, the joys of authentic, mutually fulfilling intimacy will be within your grasp.

The Signs of Narcissistic Abuse: Recognizing the Aftermath

Narcissistic abuse can leave deep and lasting scars on the psyche of its victims. Unfortunately, those who have experienced it may have difficulty recognizing the extent of the damage done because of its insidious nature. Luckily, there are several common signs and symptoms to watch out for.

Self-Doubt and Difficulty Trusting Others

One of the most pervasive effects of being in a relationship with a narcissist is developing a profound sense of self-doubt. The narcissist's toxic behavior can erode their victim's sense of self-worth and make them question their own perceptions, feelings, and desires (Durvasula, 2019).

Over time, this self-doubt can extend into your relationships with others. Having been subjected to manipulation and deceit, you may find it difficult to trust others, even those who have shown themselves to be reliable and trustworthy. You may constantly second-guess the motives and intentions of those around you, fearful of being exploited or betrayed again.

Feeling Confused and Lost

Another common sign is a sense of confusion and disorientation. The narcissist's behavior can be so erratic, unpredictable, and contradictory that you may feel like you're constantly struggling to make sense of what is happening (Bonchay, 2018).

This confusion can be particularly pronounced when your partner engages in gaslighting, which may cause you to question your memories, perceptions, and understanding of events, and make you feel unable to trust your own instincts and judgment.

Over time, this chronic state of confusion and self-doubt can leave a victim feeling utterly lost and disconnected from their own sense of self, unable to make decisions or take action with clarity or confidence.

The Long-Term Impacts of Narcissistic Abuse

Even after you've managed to break free from the narcissist's grip, the trauma of the experience can continue to reverberate through your life (Northrup, 2018). Some of the long-term impacts may include:

Difficulty forming and maintaining healthy relationships

Chronic feelings of anxiety, depression, or worthlessness

Struggles with self-esteem and self-confidence

Trust issues and difficulty opening up to others

Symptoms of post-traumatic stress disorder (PTSD)

Some may feel like they will never fully recover from the abuse suffered at the hands of a narcissist. However, with time and support, it is possible to heal and build a happier and more fulfilling life.

The Double Standards of Narcissistic Behavior

One of the hallmarks of narcissistic personality disorder (NPD) is a general sense of entitlement and a feeling of superiority to others (American Psychiatric Association, 2013). This grandiose self-image often leads the narcissist to hold others to standards of behavior and treatment that they themselves routinely violate.

In other words, narcissists often do unto others things that they would never allow to be done to themselves. They may demand complete loyalty, honesty, and devotion, while simultaneously engaging in deception, infidelity, and betrayal. They may expect their partners to cater to their every whim and desire, while showing little regard for their partner's own needs and feelings.

This double standard can cause their partners to feel like they are constantly striving to meet an impossible set of expectations. The narcissist's hypocrisy and lack of reciprocity can leave their partner feeling resentful, unappreciated, and emotionally depleted.

The Physical Toll of Narcissistic Abuse

While narcissistic abuse is primarily a form of emotional and psychological manipulation, it can also have profound physical effects on an individual. The resulting chronic stress and trauma can lead to a range of physiological symptoms and health problems, some of which may persist even after one has escaped the relationship.

As trauma expert Bessel van der Kolk (2014) explains in his book, *The Body Keeps the Score*, the effects of trauma are not just psychological, but also physiological. Regular exposure to stress and abuse can alter the body's stress response systems, leading to a range of symptoms such as:

- Chronic fatigue and exhaustion

- Headaches and muscle tension

- Gastrointestinal problems

- Insomnia and sleep disturbances

- Weakened immune system and increased susceptibility to illness

The chronic activation of the body's stress response systems can even lead to long-term changes in brain structure and function, particularly in areas related to emotion regulation, memory, and executive functioning (Bremner, 2006). These neurobiological changes can make it more difficult to process and recover from trauma, and may contribute to the development of long-term mental health problems such as depression, anxiety, and PTSD.

Recognizing the physical toll that narcissistic abuse can take is an important aspect of the healing process. It's vital to attend to your body's needs and work to regulate the physiological effects of trauma.

The Narcissist's Violation of Social Norms

Narcissistic behavior often violates the unspoken social contracts that govern our interactions with one another. Their lack of empathy, disregard for others' feelings and boundaries, and willingness to exploit and manipulate those around them are a breach of the norms of reciprocity, respect, and mutual care that underlie healthy relationships (Twenge & Campbell, 2009).

This behavior often occurs within the context of intimate, seemingly loving relationships, and can cause their partner to feel disoriented and confused about how someone who claims to love them can treat them with such callousness and disregard.

In fact, the narcissist's behavior may be so at odds with societal expectations of how a loving partner should behave that their victim may have difficulty recognizing the abuse. Many will make excuses for their partner's behavior, or blame themselves for not being understanding or accommodating enough.

The Narcissist's Exploitation of Power

Narcissists often seek out positions of power and influence, and may use their status to exploit and manipulate those around them. This can occur in a variety of contexts, from intimate relationships to the workplace to larger societal arenas.

In intimate relationships, the narcissist may use their physical, financial, or emotional power to control and dominate their partner. They may make threats, withhold resources, or engage in physical intimidation to keep their partner in line.

In the workplace, a narcissistic boss or colleague may use their position of authority to bully, belittle, or exploit their subordinates. They may take credit for others' work, shift blame for mistakes onto others, or create a toxic work environment that leaves colleagues feeling devalued and afraid.

On a societal level, narcissistic leaders and public figures may exploit their influence to shape public opinion, sow division, or consolidate their own power. They may use fear-mongering, scapegoating, or other manipulative tactics to maintain control and further their own agendas.

Recognizing the ways in which narcissists exploit power is crucial for understanding the far-reaching impacts of NPD. By naming and challenging these abuses of power, we can work to create more equitable, compassionate systems that prioritize the well-being of all individuals.

The Importance of Early Recognition

The longer you remain in a relationship with a narcissist, the more difficult it can be to escape. This is why it's crucial to be able to recognize the signs and red flags that you're in a toxic relationship as soon as possible.

Some of the early warning signs include:

- Love bombing and excessive flattery in the early stages of the relationship

- The other person has a sense of entitlement and grandiosity

- Your partner lacks empathy and dismisses others' feelings

- Your partner exhibits controlling or possessive behavior

- You experience gaslighting and other forms of manipulation

When you can identify these red flags, you can make more informed choices about your relationships. You'll be better able to set clear boundaries, trust your instincts, and find support from friends, family, and mental health professionals when needed.

And by raising awareness about the impact of narcissistic abuse, we can create a culture that is less tolerant of this form of abusive behavior and more supportive of those who have been on the receiving end of it. We can challenge the myths and misconceptions that enable narcissists to operate in all parts of life, and work to ensure that all individuals are treated with the respect, dignity, and compassion they deserve.

The Need for Self-Assessment

For too many, the process of recognizing and acknowledging the reality of their situation can be a daunting and painful one. Years of gaslighting, emotional manipulation, and psychological abuse can leave victims feeling isolated and unsure of their own perceptions and instincts. They may have internalized the narcissist's criticisms and blame, believing that they are the problem rather than the victim.

This is why the value of self-assessment and self-reflection cannot be overstated. Objectively evaluating the dynamics of your relationship will help you cut through the uncertainty, so you can see the narcissist's behavior for what it truly is. This process is not always easy, and it may bring up painful emotions and realizations, but it is an essential step on the path to healing and reclaiming your life.

In the next chapter, we will review the process of conducting a relationship self-assessment. We'll go through a comprehensive guide and questionnaire to help you evaluate the health and toxicity of your partnership. By examining key aspects of your relationship, like communication patterns, emotional reciprocity, and power dynamics, you will gain a clearer understanding of whether your partner is a narcissist.

This process is not meant to be a substitute for a professional evaluation or support, but rather a tool for increasing self-awareness and empowering you to trust your instincts and perceptions. Armed with this knowledge, you can begin your journey toward a future in which your well-being is prioritized and you're no longer at the mercy of a narcissist.

Chapter 4:
Relationship Self-Assessment Guide

In the previous chapters, we explored the characteristics of NPD, the common patterns of narcissistic abuse, and the impact that these dynamics can have on individuals in relationships with narcissists. But this behavior can be difficult to identify, especially when you are in the midst of the relationship.

This is where self-assessment comes in. By taking the time to reflect on your own experiences, feelings, and behaviors in the relationship, you can gain valuable insights into the health and dynamics of your partnership. This process can help you identify potential red flags, understand your own needs and boundaries, and make informed decisions about your future.

This Relationship Self-Assessment Guide is a structured tool for evaluating your relationship and identifying areas of concern. While this assessment is not a substitute for professional advice, it can be a helpful starting point for understanding your experiences and determining whether you may need additional support.

To begin, find a quiet, comfortable space where you can reflect on your experiences without interruptions. Set aside at least an hour to go through the questions thoughtfully and honestly. To get the most out of this self-assessment, follow these steps:

1. Set Aside Time: Find a quiet, comfortable spot where you won't be interrupted. Allocate at least an hour to go through the questions thoughtfully.

2. Be Honest: Answer each question as honestly as possible based on your experiences and feelings. There are no right or wrong answers.

3. Take Notes: Use a journal to jot down any thoughts, feelings, or memories that arise as you complete the assessment. This can provide additional insights and help you process your feelings.

4. Review and Reflect: After completing the assessment, take time to review your answers and scores. Consider what they reveal about your relationship.

The assessment consists of five parts, each focusing on different aspects of your relationship:

1. Personal Reflections

2. Your Partner's Behaviors and Traits

3. Relationship Dynamics

4. Communication Patterns

5. Future Prospects and Well-being

For each question, rate how often the statement applies to your relationship using the scale provided. Once you have completed all the questions, tally your scores for each section and use the interpretation guide to understand what your results mean.

Let's begin!

Part 1: Personal Reflections

This section focuses on your personal feelings, thoughts, and experiences within your relationship. Reflecting on your emotional state can provide crucial insights into how your relationship impacts your overall well-being.

Instructions: For each statement, rate how often it applies to your relationship on a scale from 1 to 5, where 1 = Never, 2 = Rarely, 3 = Sometimes, 4 = Often, and 5 = Always.

1. Emotional Well-being

I feel calm and comfortable around my partner.	
I feel free to express myself without walking on eggshells.	
My self-worth has improved since beginning this relationship.	
I feel energized after interactions with my partner.	
I rarely feel the need to apologize unnecessarily in my relationship.	
I feel a sense of joy and anticipation when thinking about my relationship.	
I maintain interest in activities I enjoy, with my partner's support.	
I feel proud to introduce my partner to friends and family.	
Total Score	

2. Personal Fulfillment

I feel supported and encouraged in my personal goals and ambitions.	
I feel respected and valued by my partner.	
I have a sense of independence and personal space in my relationship.	
My partner shows genuine interest in my feelings and opinions.	
I feel happy and content in my relationship.	
I feel like I can be my authentic self around my partner.	
My partner celebrates my accomplishments and successes.	
I feel a strong sense of emotional intimacy and connection with my partner.	
Total Score	

3. Conflict and Resolution

Conflicts are resolved in a healthy and constructive manner.	
I feel safe expressing my thoughts and feelings during disagreements.	
My partner listens to and considers my perspective.	
We can disagree without it turning into a major argument.	
I feel heard and understood after a disagreement.	
My partner takes responsibility for their actions and apologizes when appropriate.	
We're able to find compromises and solutions that work for both of us.	
I feel closer to my partner after resolving conflicts, rather than resentful or disconnected.	
Total Score	

4. Self-Perception and Autonomy

I feel confident in my decision-making abilities in the relationship.	
I am able to maintain my own interests and friendships outside of the relationship.	
I feel comfortable setting boundaries and saying "no" when I want to.	
My partner respects my privacy and does not invade my personal space.	
I feel like an equal partner in the relationship, not controlled or dominated.	
I am able to express my opinions and beliefs without fear of ridicule or retribution.	
I feel like my partner trusts me and does not exhibit excessive jealousy or possessiveness.	
I have a strong sense of self-identity and do not feel like I am losing myself in my relationship.	
Total Score	

Scoring for Part 1:

Add up your scores for each statement. Higher scores indicate a healthier relationship dynamic.

Interpreting Your Score:

- (128-160) Low Risk: Your relationship generally demonstrates healthy dynamics in these areas.

- (96-127) Moderate Risk: There are some concerns in these areas that may need attention.

- (32-95) High Risk: These areas show significant issues that require immediate attention and possibly professional help.

Remember that these results should be considered alongside the other parts of the assessment and should not be used as a definitive diagnosis. If you have concerns about your relationship based on your scores, it may be helpful to seek the guidance of a qualified therapist or counselor.

Part 2: Partner's Behaviors and Traits

This section assesses your partner's behaviors and traits, focusing on identifying healthy relationship patterns and potential problematic behaviors.

Instructions: For each statement, rate how often it applies to your partner on a scale from 1 to 5, where 1 = Never, 2 = Rarely, 3 = Sometimes, 4 = Often, and 5 = Always.

1. Self-Assurance and Humility

My partner is comfortable with themselves without needing constant admiration from others.	
My partner acknowledges their achievements without expecting excessive recognition.	
My partner is gracious when they don't receive special treatment.	
My partner appreciates and celebrates others' achievements and contributions.	
My partner treats others as equals, without a sense of superiority.	
My partner is content with quiet accomplishments without seeking constant praise.	
My partner responds well to constructive feedback and criticism.	
My partner respects my needs and desires as equally important to their own.	
Total Score	

2. Empathy and Understanding

My partner makes an effort to understand and acknowledge my feelings.	
My partner listens attentively without interrupting during conversations.	
My partner shows genuine interest in my needs and concerns.	
My partner responds calmly and supportively when I express my emotions.	
My partner validates my experiences and perspectives.	
My partner shows empathy and offers support during difficult times.	
My partner sincerely apologizes and takes responsibility for their hurtful actions.	
My partner considers how situations affect me as well as themselves.	
Total Score	

3. Respect for Autonomy

My partner respects my right to make my own decisions and choices.	
My partner communicates their wants without using guilt or manipulation.	
My partner takes responsibility for their actions without shifting blame.	
My partner expresses their needs without using threats or intimidation.	
My partner encourages my relationships with friends and family.	
My partner respects my privacy and personal boundaries.	
My partner values my perceptions and memories as valid.	
My partner expresses affection and support consistently, not as a means of control.	
Total Score	

4. Mutual Consideration

My partner believes in equal treatment and privileges in our relationship.	
My partner reciprocates care and support in our relationship.	
My partner contributes fairly to our shared time, resources, and responsibilities.	
My partner respects my boundaries and personal space.	
My partner uses their charm or charisma positively, not for manipulation.	
My partner includes me in decision-making processes that affect our relationship.	
My partner is protective of my vulnerabilities and doesn't exploit them.	
My partner believes in a balance of needs and desires in our relationship.	
Total Score	

Scoring for Part 2:

Add up the scores for each statement within each subsection. Higher scores indicate healthier relationship dynamics and fewer narcissistic tendencies.

Interpreting Results:

- (128-160) Low Risk: Your partner generally demonstrates healthy behaviors and traits in these areas.

- (96-127) Moderate Risk: There are some concerns in these areas that may need attention.

- (32-95) High Risk: These areas show significant issues that require immediate attention and possibly professional help.

Remember that while these results can provide valuable insights, they should not be used as a definitive diagnosis. If you have concerns about your partner's behavior based on your scores, it could be beneficial to seek the guidance of a qualified mental health professional who can provide a more comprehensive assessment and support.

Part 3: Relationship Dynamics

This section evaluates the overall dynamics and health of your relationship, focusing on how both of you contribute to the relationship.

Instructions: For each statement, rate how often it applies to your relationship on a scale from 1 to 5, where 1 = Never, 2 = Rarely, 3 = Sometimes, 4 = Often, and 5 = Always.

1. Balance and Equality

Both partners contribute equally to the relationship.	
Decisions are made together, with both of us having an equal say.	
Both of us take responsibility for maintaining the relationship.	
There is mutual respect and consideration in our relationship.	
Both partners have an equal voice in discussing and resolving issues.	
Our relationship feels like a true partnership, with both of us working together.	
We are both willing to compromise and find mutually beneficial solutions.	
The distribution of household tasks and responsibilities feels fair and balanced.	
Total Score	

2. Support and Encouragement

We support each other's personal growth and ambitions.	
We celebrate each other's successes and accomplishments.	
We each provide emotional support for the other during difficult times.	
We both encourage open and honest communication.	
We are both genuinely interested in each other's lives and well-being.	
Both of us offer encouragement and motivation when our partner is facing challenges.	
Together we have created a safe and non-judgmental space for sharing feelings and experiences.	
Both of us actively listen and provide empathy and understanding to the other.	
Total Score	

3. Trust and Security

I feel secure and confident in the stability of our relationship.	
We trust each other and feel trusted.	
We respect each other's privacy and boundaries.	
We both feel a strong sense of loyalty toward the other.	
We are both transparent and honest about our thoughts, feelings, and actions.	
Both of us follow through on the commitments and promises we make to each other.	
We both feel comfortable being vulnerable and sharing our fears and insecurities.	
Our relationship provides a sense of emotional safety and security.	
Total Score	

4. Mutual Respect and Appreciation

We each treat each other with kindness, respect, and dignity.	
We express gratitude and appreciation for each other's efforts and contributions.	
We both value and respect each other's opinions, even when we disagree.	
We both acknowledge and apologize for our mistakes or hurtful actions.	
Both of us make an effort to understand and accommodate the other's needs and preferences.	
We speak positively about each other in front of others.	
We respect each other's individual identity and autonomy within our relationship.	
We both show respect for each other's family, friends, and personal interests.	
Total Score	

Scoring for Part 3:

Add up the scores for each statement within each subsection. Higher scores in each subsection indicate a healthier and more balanced relationship dynamic.

Interpreting Results:

- (128-160) Low Risk: Your relationship demonstrates strong, healthy dynamics in these areas.

- (96-127) Moderate Risk: There are some areas that could benefit from improvement. Consider discussing these with your partner.

- (32-95) High Risk: These areas show significant issues that require attention. Consider seeking professional help to address these concerns.

Lower scores in any subsection may indicate areas of the relationship that could benefit from greater and more open communication between partners. If you consistently score low across multiple subsections, you might consider further exploring these dynamics with your partner or even seeking guidance from a relationship counselor or therapist.

Part 4: Communication Patterns

Effective communication is the foundation of any healthy relationship. This section evaluates how conflicts are handled in your relationship and the styles of communication that are used.

Instructions: For each statement, rate how often it applies to your relationship on a scale from 1 to 5, where 1 = Never, 2 = Rarely, 3 = Sometimes, 4 = Often, and 5 = Always.

1. Conflict Resolution

We address conflicts calmly and respectfully.	
Both of us are willing to compromise during disagreements.	
We avoid name-calling or personal attacks during arguments.	
We can discuss sensitive topics without having it escalate into a fight.	
Both of us take responsibility for our actions during conflicts.	
We focus on finding solutions rather than assigning blame.	
We take breaks when necessary to prevent disagreements from escalating.	
After a conflict, we both apologize sincerely and work to make amends.	
Total Score	

2. Active Listening

My partner listens attentively when I speak.	
My partner acknowledges my feelings and concerns.	
We both make an effort to understand each other's perspectives.	
Interruptions are rare during our conversations.	
We often repeat back what we heard to ensure we understand what the other has said.	
We both ask questions to gain clarity and show interest in what the other person is saying.	
We maintain eye contact and use non-verbal cues to show we are engaged in the conversation.	
We create a safe and non-judgmental space for each other to express ourselves.	
Total Score	

3. Expression of Needs

I feel comfortable expressing my needs and desires.	
My partner respects and considers my needs.	
We regularly check in with each other about our needs and feelings.	
We encourage each other to express our true selves.	
We handle misunderstandings with patience and empathy.	
We use "I" statements to express our feelings and needs clearly and non-defensively.	
We make an effort to understand and validate each other's needs, even if we can't always meet them.	
We work together to find mutually satisfying ways to address each other's needs.	
Total Score	

4. Emotional Openness and Vulnerability

I feel safe being emotionally open and vulnerable with my partner.	
My partner shares their own emotions and vulnerabilities with me.	
We create a non-judgmental and supportive space for each other to express our feelings.	
We validate and empathize with each other's emotions, even if we don't fully understand them.	
We are both patient and understanding when the other is struggling to express their emotions.	
We use emotional check-ins to stay connected and attuned to each other's feelings.	
We offer comfort and reassurance to each other during emotionally challenging times.	
We celebrate and appreciate moments of emotional intimacy and connection.	
Total Score	

Scoring for Part 4:

Add up the scores for each statement within each subsection. Higher scores in each subsection indicate healthier communication patterns and more effective conflict resolution skills.

Interpreting Results:

- (128-160) Low Risk: Your relationship demonstrates strong, healthy communication patterns in these areas.

- (96-127) Moderate Risk: There are some areas of communication that could benefit from improvement. Consider discussing these with your partner.

- (32-95) High Risk: These areas show significant communication issues that require attention. Consider seeking professional help to address these concerns.

Lower scores in any subsection may indicate areas of communication that could benefit from targeted skill-building. If you consistently score low across multiple subsections, it may be helpful to further explore these communication patterns with your partner or seek the guidance of a couples therapist or communication specialist.

Part 5: Future Prospects and Well-being

This section encourages you to consider the future of your relationship and its impact on your personal well-being.

Instructions: For each statement, rate how often it applies to your relationship on a scale from 1 to 5, where 1 = Never, 2 = Rarely, 3 = Sometimes, 4 = Often, and 5 = Always.

1. Vision for the Future

I can envision a positive future with my partner.	
We often talk about our long-term goals and plans.	
We are both committed to a shared future.	
Our visions for the future align well with each other.	
We support each other's aspirations and dreams.	
We make decisions with our shared future in mind.	
We are excited about the prospect of growing old together.	
We have discussed and are aligned on important future topics (e.g., marriage, children, finances).	
Total Score	

2. Personal Well-being

I feel healthier and happier since entering into this relationship.	
My partner encourages me to take care of myself.	
I feel a strong sense of personal growth within this relationship.	
My partner supports my mental and emotional well-being.	
My relationship has a positive influence on my life, rather than causing stress.	
I have maintained a sense of self and autonomy while being in this relationship.	
My partner encourages me to pursue my passions and interests.	
I feel more resilient and capable of handling life's challenges with my partner's support.	
Total Score	

3. Mutual Satisfaction

Both of us express satisfaction with our relationship.	
We regularly discuss and adjust our relationship dynamics to ensure mutual happiness.	
We celebrate our relationship milestones and achievements.	
We both feel fulfilled and valued in our relationship.	
My partner and I have a strong and satisfying physical and emotional connection.	
We prioritize quality time together and make an effort to keep the spark alive.	
We express gratitude for each other and for each other's contributions to the relationship.	
We have a shared sense of humor and enjoy making each other laugh.	
Total Score	

4. Personal Growth and Development

My partner encourages and supports my personal growth and development.	
I feel inspired to become a better version of myself because of my relationship.	
We challenge each other to step outside our comfort zones and try new things.	
We have open and honest conversations about our individual goals and how we can support each other.	
We celebrate each other's achievements and milestones, both big and small.	
We create a safe space for each other to be vulnerable and share our fears and insecurities.	
We provide constructive feedback and guidance to help each other grow and improve.	
Our relationship has helped me develop greater self-awareness and emotional intelligence.	
Total Score	

Scoring for Part 5:

Add up the scores for each statement within each subsection. Higher scores in each subsection indicate a more positive outlook for the future of your relationship and a greater positive impact on your personal well-being and growth.

Interpreting Results:

- (128-160) Low Risk: Your relationship demonstrates strong, positive prospects for the future and contributes significantly to your personal well-being and growth.

- (96-127) Moderate Risk: There are some areas regarding your future prospects or personal well-being that could benefit from improvement. Consider discussing these with your partner.

- (32-95) High Risk: These areas show significant concerns about your relationship's future or its impact on your well-being. Consider seeking professional help to address these issues.

Remember, this assessment is a tool for self-reflection and should not be used as a definitive measure of your relationship's future prospects or its impact on your well-being. If you have concerns about your relationship's trajectory or its effect on your personal growth, it's always beneficial to discuss them openly with your partner or seek guidance from a qualified relationship counselor or therapist.

Lower scores in any subsection may indicate areas where your relationship's long-term prospects or its impact on your well-being could be improved. If you consistently score low across multiple subsections, you may find it worthwhile to reflect on your relationship's trajectory and discuss your concerns and hopes for the future with your partner. If you find it difficult to have these conversations or feel that your personal growth and well-being are being compromised, it may be beneficial to seek the guidance of a relationship counselor or therapist.

Calculating Your Score

After completing each part of the self-assessment, add up the scores for each statement within that section. The total score for each section will help you understand the dynamics and potential concerns in that particular area of your relationship.

Interpreting Your Score

For all parts of the assessment:

- (128-160) Low Risk: Your relationship generally demonstrates healthy dynamics in this area.

- (96-127) Moderate Risk: There are some concerns in this area that may need attention.

- (32-95) High Risk: This area shows significant issues that require immediate attention and possibly professional help.

Part 1: Personal Reflections Score:

- Low Risk (128-160): You generally feel positive, secure, and emotionally fulfilled in your relationship. Your partner respects your individuality and supports your well-being.

- Moderate Risk (96-127): There are some emotional concerns and areas that need improvement. Consider discussing these issues with your partner and exploring ways to enhance emotional intimacy and personal fulfillment.

- High Risk (32-95): You are experiencing significant emotional distress and dissatisfaction in your relationship. It is important to prioritize your well-being and seek support from a therapist or counselor to address these concerns and evaluate the health of your relationship.

Part 2: Partner's Behaviors and Traits Score:

- Low Risk (128-160): Your partner's behaviors and traits are generally healthy and supportive. They demonstrate empathy, respect, and a willingness to take responsibility for their actions.

- Moderate Risk (96-127): Some of your partner's behaviors or traits may indicate concerning patterns. It is important to monitor these behaviors and address them with your partner to prevent further escalation.

- High Risk (32-95): Your partner exhibits a high number of problematic behaviors and traits, which can be emotionally damaging and harmful to your well-being. It is crucial to prioritize your own safety and well-being, and seek professional support to evaluate the viability of the relationship.

Part 3: Relationship Dynamics Score:

- High Score (128-160): Your relationship demonstrates a healthy balance of power, mutual support, trust, and respect. Both of you contribute equally to maintaining a positive and fulfilling relationship.

- Moderate Score (96-127): There are some imbalances or areas that need improvement in your relationship dynamics. Focus on enhancing equality, support, trust, and mutual respect.

- Low Score (32-95): Your relationship exhibits significant issues in terms of power dynamics, lack of support, trust, or respect. These concerns should be addressed promptly, perhaps even with the help of a relationship counselor or therapist, who can help you improve the overall health and functioning of your relationship.

Part 4: Communication Patterns Score:

a) High Score (128-160): You and your partner demonstrate effective, respectful, and emotionally attuned communication. Conflicts are resolved constructively, and both of you feel heard and understood.

b) Moderate Score (96-127): There are some communication issues or areas that could use improvement. Focus on enhancing active listening skills, expressing needs and emotions effectively, and developing healthier conflict resolution strategies.

c) Low Score (32-95): Your relationship appears to have major communication problems, such as a lack of emotional openness, poor conflict resolution, and failure to listen and understand each other's perspectives. Professional help from a couples therapist or communication specialist may be necessary to develop more effective communication patterns.

Part 5: Future Prospects and Well-being Score:

- High Score (128-160): You and your partner have a positive outlook for the future, with a strong sense of shared goals, mutual satisfaction, and personal growth within your relationship.

- Moderate Score (96-127): There are some concerns or areas that need improvement regarding the overall impact of the relationship on your well-being. Discuss these concerns with your partner and explore ways to better align your goals and support each other's personal development.

- Low Score (32-95): You have significant doubts about the future of your relationship and its ability to support your personal growth and well-being. It is important to prioritize your own needs and consider seeking professional guidance to evaluate the long-term viability of the relationship.

**Disclaimer: This self-assessment guide is intended for informational purposes only and should not be considered a substitute for professional advice. If you are experiencing significant distress or abuse in your relationship, please seek support from a qualified therapist or counselor.

Now that you have completed the self-assessment and have a better understanding of your relationship dynamics, take some time to reflect on your results and consider the next steps in your journey.

If your scores indicate a generally healthy and positive relationship, celebrate all that you and your partner have built together. Continue to nurture and maintain the positive aspects of your relationship, while also remaining mindful of areas that may need ongoing attention and growth. Regularly checking in with each other, practicing open and honest communication, and prioritizing mutual support and respect can help you maintain a strong and fulfilling partnership throughout your life together.

If your scores suggest there are concerns or areas that could use improvement, it's important to proactively address these. Consider setting aside dedicated time to discuss your thoughts and feelings with your partner. Approach these conversations with openness, empathy, and a willingness to listen and understand each other's perspectives. Work together to identify specific steps you can take to enhance the health and happiness of your relationship, such as improving communication skills, setting healthy boundaries, or seeking support from a couples therapist or relationship coach.

If your scores indicate a high risk of narcissistic behaviors from your partner or other significant relationship issues, it's time to prioritize your own well-being and safety. Seeking support from a qualified mental health professional, perhaps even someone who specializes in narcissistic abuse recovery, can provide you with guidance, validation, and coping strategies. Remember, you are not alone, and there are resources and support systems available to help you navigate this challenging situation.

The insights gained from this self-assessment are a valuable starting point in your journey toward greater self-awareness, personal growth, and a healthier, more satisfying relationship. Use this knowledge as a foundation for ongoing reflection, communication, and action, and trust in your ability to create positive change in your life and relationships.

Chapter 5:
Breaking Free from Narcissistic Influence

"The first step in breaking free from a narcissist's control is to recognize that you are being controlled." - Ramani Durvasula, Author of *Should I Stay or Should I Go?*

Sarah sat at her kitchen table, staring sadly at the self-assessment guide she had just completed. The results were clear: her relationship with David exhibited numerous signs of narcissistic abuse. As she reflected on the past few years, she began to recognize the patterns – the constant criticism, the gaslighting, the emotional manipulation. She had always made excuses for David's behavior, convincing herself that he would change or that she was overreacting. But now, with the evidence laid out in front of her, Sarah could no longer deny the truth.

For Sarah, the self-assessment guide was a turning point. It validated her experiences and gave her the courage to confront the reality of her situation. She realized that she was not alone and that there was hope for her future. But she also knew that the road ahead would not be easy, because she knew that narcissists can make leaving seem impossible.

If you've found yourself in a similar situation to Sarah's, having completed the self-assessment guide and recognized the signs of narcissistic abuse in your relationship, you're probably feeling a mix of emotions – fear, confusion, and uncertainty about what to do next. Freeing yourself from a narcissist's influence requires courage, support, and a full understanding of the tactics they use to maintain control.

According to a study by the National Coalition Against Domestic Violence, nearly half of all women and men in the United States have experienced psychological aggression from an intimate partner in their lifetime (NCADV, 2021). This staggering statistic highlights the pervasive nature of emotional abuse and manipulation in relationships.

In this chapter, we'll learn about strategies you can employ to break free from narcissistic abuse and reclaim your autonomy. We'll discuss the challenges that arise when leaving a narcissist and provide practical tips for navigating this difficult transition. Whether you're currently in a relationship with a narcissist or have recently left one, this chapter will provide you with the tools and knowledge you need to move forward and create a life free from the toxicity that a narcissist brings to a relationship.

So, where should you start? It begins with recognizing the influence the narcissist has over you and taking the steps necessary to free yourself and forge a new path forward.

Unmasking the Narcissist: Undoing the Brainwashing

One of the most important things to recognize is that the person you fell in love with is not the person you know today, but was a carefully crafted façade designed to evoke a specific emotional response from you.

The Narcissist's Persona: A Mirage of Deception

As we've learned, at the core of every narcissist is an insatiable need for attention, admiration, and control. To achieve this, they create a persona that is tailored to draw in their victims and keep them emotionally invested in the relationship. This persona is a mirage, a deceptive illusion that can be incredibly difficult to see through.

Narcissists are highly skilled at reading their audience and adapting their behavior to elicit the response they desire. They can be charming, charismatic, and attentive, making their victims feel special, loved, and understood, but this is merely a calculated manipulation designed to serve their own needs and desires.

As Dr. Durvasula tells us, "Narcissists are con artists. They are always scanning their environment for prey and looking for people they can manipulate. They are masters at reading people and understanding what makes them tick" (Durvasula, 2019).

The Competitive Nature of Narcissists

Another trait of narcissists is their intense competitiveness. They crave opportunities to showcase their superiority and to be seen as the best at everything they do. This often manifests in grandiose claims and a constant need to one-up others.

Narcissists may boast about their achievements, their possessions, or their status, always seeking to position themselves as the most successful, the most talented, or the most intelligent. They may even enter the realm of victimhood, claiming to have suffered more than anyone else or to have overcome the greatest challenges.

Dr. Craig Malkin, author of *Rethinking Narcissism*, notes, "Narcissists are always trying to win, to be seen as special and unique. They need to feel superior to others, and they'll go to great lengths to maintain that sense of superiority, even if it means lying, cheating, or exploiting others" (Malkin, 2015).

The Limitations of Clinical Definitions

While there are clinical criteria for diagnosing NPD, these definitions often fall short in capturing the full range of narcissistic behaviors and traits. Many of those who exhibit narcissistic tendencies may not meet the full diagnostic criteria for the disorder, but can still cause significant harm to others.

Also, the clinical definition of NPD tends to focus on overt, grandiose narcissism, which is characterized by bold, self-aggrandizing behavior and a sense of entitlement. However, as we discussed earlier, there is a form of narcissism known as covert or vulnerable narcissism, which is more subtle and harder to detect.

Covert narcissists may present as shy, sensitive, or even self-deprecating, but beneath this exterior lies the same core traits of entitlement, competitiveness, and a lack of empathy. They may use more subtle forms of manipulation, such as playing the victim or using passive-aggression to control their partners.

Recognizing the Red Flags

One of the most common red flags of narcissism is when someone makes grandiose claims or positions themselves as the best or most important person in any given situation. Narcissists tend to use superlatives to describe themselves, their accomplishments, or their experiences.

For example, a narcissistic partner may claim to be the best lover you've ever had, the most successful person in their field, or the most intelligent person in any room. They may also present themselves as a victim who has suffered more than anyone else or who's had to overcome incredible obstacles.

If you find yourself nodding in recognition as you read this, it may be that you are in a relationship with a narcissistic individual. Just remember to trust your instincts and pay attention to any feelings of unease or discomfort that arise in response to your partner's behavior.

The Double Life of Narcissists

Another common feature of narcissistic relationships is the discovery that your partner has been living a double life. Narcissists are skilled at compartmentalizing their lives and keeping their various personas separate from one another.

They may present one face to their partner, another to their colleagues or friends, and yet another to their family or community. This can cause cognitive dissonance for their partners, who may struggle to reconcile the different versions of their partner.

In extreme cases, narcissists may even lead entirely separate lives, with multiple partners, families, or careers that they keep hidden from one another. Naturally, such a discovery is devastating for their victims, who feel betrayed, confused, and begin to question their own reality.

One example of this is the case of Dr. Paolo Macchiarini, a renowned transplant surgeon who was featured in a Netflix documentary called *Bad Surgeon*. Macchiarini presented himself as a pioneering surgeon and innovator in the field of regenerative medicine. He claimed to have developed groundbreaking techniques for creating artificial tracheas using stem cells and synthetic scaffolds. But as it turned out, Macchiarini was a fraud. He'd falsified data, misrepresented his surgical outcomes, and exploited vulnerable patients who were desperate for life-saving treatments. He also engaged in a series of romantic relationships with women, often leading them to believe that he was single and promising them a future together, while in reality he was already married with children.

Though extreme, the story of Paolo Macchiarini is a disturbing example of how narcissists can use their positions of power and influence to manipulate and deceive others, causing immense harm to their victims and undermining the trust placed in them by society.

Understanding the Narcissist's Mind Games

Narcissists employ a variety of subtle and insidious mind games to brainwash and control their victims. These tactics create cognitive dissonance, a state of mental confusion and distress that arises when a person's beliefs, values, or perceptions are challenged by contradictory information or experiences.

Understanding these mind games is an important step toward protecting yourself from their influence.

A. Pretending Not to Understand Basic Societal Norms and Morals

One common tactic used by narcissists is to feign ignorance or confusion about basic social norms, values, and moral principles. They may act as though they don't understand why certain behaviors are inappropriate or hurtful, even when it is clear that they are violating established boundaries or causing harm to others.

This destabilizes their victims and causes them to question their own understanding of those norms and values. By presenting themselves as innocent, narcissists can avoid taking responsibility for their actions and shift the blame onto others, who often begin to doubt their own judgment and perceptions.

B. Deflecting and Attacking: The "What About-ism" Strategy

When confronted with their hurtful or manipulative behavior, narcissists often resort to a tactic known as "deflecting and attacking." Rather than acknowledging their own actions or taking responsibility for their mistakes, they will quickly turn the tables on their accuser, shifting the focus onto their perceived flaws or wrongdoings.

This strategy, also known as "what about-ism," involves responding to criticism or accusations with counter-accusations or irrelevant distractions. For example, if a victim confronts their narcissistic partner about their controlling behavior, the narcissist may respond by bringing up a past mistake or transgression of the victim, effectively derailing the conversation and avoiding accountability.

C.   Deny, Deny, Deny

Narcissists also engage in denial and distraction. When confronted with evidence of their hurtful or manipulative behavior, they often deny any wrongdoing, even in the face of clear proof or multiple witnesses. This can be incredibly disorienting for victims, who may then question their own memories, perceptions, and understanding of events. Narcissists may even couple their denials with distractions or counter-accusations, which can further destabilize their victims.

Over time, this persistent denial and distraction can lead to gaslighting, which we've talked about many times already. In extreme circumstances, a victim may begin to feel like they're losing their grip on the truth or blame themselves for the problems in the relationship.

D.   The Psychic Reading: Telling You How You Feel

Narcissists also may behave as if they already know what's in their victim's hearts and minds, making pronouncements about what their partner is thinking or feeling, even when they have no way of knowing.

For example, they may say things like, "I know you're still hung up on your ex," or "You're just angry because you're jealous of my success." These statements are often designed to provoke an emotional response and to keep the other person off-balance and questioning their real feelings.

By claiming to know someone else's inner world better than the person knows it themselves, narcissists can maintain a sense of control and superiority in the relationship. Tactics like this can be used to dismiss or invalidate their partner's feelings, or to manipulate them into behaving in ways that serve the narcissist's own interests.

E.   Reframing Reality: The Ultimate Manipulation

One of the most insidious mind games employed by narcissists is when they attempt to reframe reality. When confronted with a situation that threatens their sense of control or superiority, they may try to reframe the entire narrative in a way that serves their own interests.

For example, if their partner tries to address a specific problem or concern in their relationship, a narcissist may shift the conversation to a completely different topic, such as their partner's past relationships or even their shortcomings. This can derail any conversation and helps the narcissist avoid taking responsibility for their behavior.

Reframing can also be used to twist someone's words or intentions, making it seem as though the victim is the one at fault or is being unreasonable, which again can cause them to doubt their own judgment and perceptions.

The Emotional Manipulation at the Heart of Narcissistic Abuse

All these mind games illustrate that narcissistic abuse is not about the narcissist themselves, but about the emotional responses they can elicit from their victims. They feed off of the emotional reactions of those around them, using fear, guilt, shame, and confusion to maintain their sense of power and control. They may provoke arguments or conflicts simply to get a rise out of their partner, or may use love bombing and idealization to keep their partner fully invested in the relationship.

Additional Narcissistic Tactics

In addition to all the strategies discussed so far, narcissists have other means to control, confuse, and exploit their victims. Below we will unveil a few more methods that you must be able to recognize in order to keep it from being used on you.

Triangulation

Triangulation is when the narcissist brings a third person into the dynamic of your relationship, often to create jealousy, insecurity, or a sense of competition. This third person could be an ex-partner, a friend, or even a complete stranger. By constantly comparing their current partner to others or hinting at the possibility of infidelity, narcissists can keep their victims in a state of constant anxiety and self-doubt.

The Fake Apology

Narcissists are notorious for their insincere apologies. When confronted with their hurtful behavior, they may offer a superficial apology that lacks genuine remorse or accountability. These apologies often come with qualifiers, like blaming the victim or minimizing the impact of their behavior. By offering fake apologies, narcissists create the illusion of taking responsibility while still maintaining their sense of superiority and control.

Boundary Pushing

Narcissists have a fundamental disregard for the boundaries and autonomy of others. They often push against their partner's boundaries, whether it be through excessive demands on their time and energy, invasions of privacy, or disrespect for personal space. By eroding their victim's boundaries over time, narcissists stoke feelings of helplessness and make it increasingly difficult for their victims to assert their own needs and desires.

Fault-Finding

Nothing is ever good enough for a narcissist. They are perpetually on the lookout for flaws, mistakes, or shortcomings in their partners, which they can then use as ammunition for criticism and blame. This constant fault-finding can erode their partner's self-esteem and make them feel like they will never measure up to the narcissist's impossible standards.

Mirroring

In the early stages of a relationship, narcissists often engage in mirroring. They will closely observe their victim's interests, preferences, and communication style, and then reflect these back to create a sense of connection and compatibility. This mirroring can be incredibly seductive, because it makes people feel understood and appreciated, but it is merely a means to create a superficial bond of intimacy and trust.

Projection

Narcissists commonly use projection, which involves attributing their own negative qualities or behaviors onto their victims. For example, a narcissist who is prone to infidelity may constantly accuse their partner of cheating, or one who is deeply insecure may accuse their partner of being needy or clingy. By projecting their own flaws onto others, narcissists can avoid taking responsibility for their actions and maintain their own feelings of superiority and righteousness.

Virtue-Signaling

Narcissists often present themselves as paragons of virtue, morality, and righteousness. They may engage in public acts of charity, social justice activism, or religious devotion, all while engaging in abusive or manipulative behavior behind closed doors. This is called virtue-signaling, which helps them build a positive public image and often makes their victims feel guilty or inadequate for questioning their behavior.

Withholding Affection

Narcissists may use affection and attention as a weapon, withholding it as a form of punishment or control. If their partner displeases them or fails to meet their expectations, they may suddenly become cold, distant, or unavailable. This intermittent reinforcement can be incredibly confusing and distressing for victims, who may blame themselves for the narcissist's withdrawal and work harder to regain their favor.

Do You Recognize These Tactics in Your Partner?

As you read through the list of narcissistic tactics above, you may have found yourself nodding in recognition or feeling a sense of unease. Perhaps your partner has even used some of these strategies. Take a moment to reflect on your relationship. Have you noticed your partner presenting one face to the world while behaving differently behind closed doors? Do they regularly claim to be the best at something, whether it's their professional achievements, their intellect, or even their suffering?

If you've identified a pattern of these tactics being used by your partner, trust your instincts and consider your options for preventing them from doing you any further harm.

Breaking Free: The 5 Keys

So, how can you break free from the narcissist's influence and mind games? It starts with understanding 5 key points:

1. Know Who They Really Are

At their core, narcissists' primary goal is to induce emotional responses in their victims, whether it be fear, guilt, shame, or confusion. By recognizing this, you can begin to identify their behavior for what it is: manipulation designed to keep you off-balance and under their control.

2. Break the Cycle of Action and Reaction

Narcissists thrive on the cycle of action and reaction. They provoke an emotional response from their victims, which in turn triggers a reaction that the narcissist can then use to further their own agenda. To break this cycle, you must learn to detach from their stimulus and respond in a measured, intentional way.

3. Be Goal-Oriented in Your Interactions

Remember that you are never truly communicating with a narcissist in the way you would with a healthy partner. They are always working toward an underlying agenda or goal. Approach interactions with a clear sense of purpose and boundaries as you focus on maintaining your emotional equilibrium and achieving your objectives.

4. Play the Game

Narcissists view relationships as a game to be won, and they are skilled at using manipulation tactics to keep others on the defensive. To level the playing field, you may need to learn to play their game. This doesn't mean engaging in abusive behavior yourself, but using strategic communication and boundary-setting to keep them off-balance and less able to control the situation.

5. Use Manipulation for Self-Protection

One of the most effective ways to combat narcissistic abuse is to use manipulation tactics in reverse. This may feel uncomfortable or even unethical at first, but remember that you are using these strategies to protect yourself, not to inflict harm. By setting clear goals for your interactions and using strategic communication techniques, you can begin to reclaim your autonomy and establish healthier boundaries.

To effectively employ these strategies, it's crucial to understand both your own strengths and weaknesses and those of the narcissist. What are your emotional triggers? What are your non-negotiable boundaries? What are the narcissist's patterns of behavior and methods of manipulation? By gaining clarity on these points, you'll be able to develop a more strategic approach to your interactions with your partner. You can learn to anticipate their moves, respond in a way that maintains your own emotional stability, and gradually disentangle yourself from their web of control.

Chapter 6:
Techniques to End the
Gaslighting and Manipulative Tactics

*The Art of Turning the Tables: A Historical
Example of Defeating Narcissistic Manipulation*

*In the early 1900s, the world was captivated by the rise of a new kind
of leader - the charismatic, ruthless, and unapologetically narcissistic
tyrant. One such figure was Benito Mussolini, the fascist dictator who
ruled Italy with an iron fist from 1922 to 1943.*

*Mussolini was a master of manipulation, using his oratory skills and
propaganda machine to create a cult of personality around himself. He
portrayed himself as a savior of the Italian people, a man of destiny
who could lead the nation to greatness. He promised to restore Italy's
former glory and to make the trains run on time.*

*However, behind the façade of strength and unity, Mussolini was a
deeply insecure and paranoid man. He surrounded himself with
sycophants and yes-men, and he brutally suppressed any opposition
to his rule. He used violence, intimidation, and manipulation to
maintain his grip on power.*

*One of the few people who saw through Mussolini was a young
journalist named Indro Montanelli. Montanelli was assigned to
interview Mussolini in 1935, and he quickly realized that the dictator
was not the all-powerful figure he claimed to be.*

Instead of being intimidated by Mussolini's bluster and bravado, Montanelli remained calm and unimpressed. He asked pointed questions that exposed the flaws in Mussolini's logic and the inconsistencies in his rhetoric. He refused to be drawn into Mussolini's mind games or to be swayed by his charm.

Montanelli's approach was a master class in how to deal with a narcissistic manipulator. He recognized that Mussolini's power relied on the illusion of infallibility, and he set out to shatter that illusion. He didn't engage in sincere communication or attempt to appeal to Mussolini's better nature. Instead, he played the game on his own terms, using wit, intelligence, and strategic questioning to expose the man behind the curtain.

In the end, Montanelli's interview with Mussolini became a turning point in the dictator's reign. It showed the Italian people that their leader was not invincible, and it planted the seeds of doubt that would eventually lead to Mussolini's downfall.

The lesson of Montanelli's encounter with Mussolini is clear: when dealing with a narcissist, one must abandon the notion of sincere communication and instead focus on strategic interaction. By recognizing the game being played and refusing to be drawn into the narcissist's web, it is possible to turn the tables and expose the true nature of their character.

Recognizing Manipulation: The First Step to Freedom

One of the greatest challenges in dealing with narcissistic manipulation is simply recognizing it for what it is. As we've learned, narcissists are masters of disguise, able to present a charming and persuasive façade that can fool even the most discerning individuals.

This is why so much of this book has been dedicated to exploring the techniques and psychology behind narcissism. By understanding the tactics used by narcissists - such as gaslighting, love bombing, and triangulation - you can dispel the fog of confusion and self-doubt that often accompanies these relationships.

It's important to remember that narcissists do not engage in manipulation accidentally or unconsciously. They are deliberate and calculating in their actions as they strive to maintain control and feed their insatiable need for admiration and validation.

So you must recognize it for what it is - a deliberate attempt to undermine your sense of reality and keep you trapped in a cycle of abuse.

Abandoning Sincere Communication: Playing the Game on Your Own Terms

Once you recognize the tactics your partner is using, you need to let go of the idea that you can engage in sincere communication with your narcissistic partner. This can be a difficult and painful realization, especially if you have invested a great deal of time and emotion into the relationship. But it's important to remind yourself that narcissists do not engage in relationships in the same way that healthy people do. For them, relationships are a means to an end, a way to have what they crave and maintain their fragile sense of self.

This is why sincere, heartfelt communication with a narcissist is often an exercise in futility. They will use your vulnerabilities against you, twisting your words and manipulating your emotions to keep you under their control. Instead, you might want to try playing their game but on your own terms. This means reducing your emotional reactivity and giving them less to work with.

Some suggestions on how to accomplish this include:

- Giving shorter, more concise responses to their attempts at engagement

- Refusing to be drawn into circular arguments or debates

- Avoiding sharing your deepest feelings or vulnerabilities

- Maintaining a calm, neutral demeanor when they attempt to provoke you

By disrupting the cycle of manipulation, you can start to regain some control over your life.

Of course, this is easier said than done, especially in the heat of the moment when emotions are running high. It takes practice, patience, and a great deal of self-awareness to change the patterns of interaction in a narcissistic relationship.

Strategies to Combat the Narcissist

1. Reducing the Narcissist's Significance in Your Life

If you can genuinely shift your focus and priorities away from the narcissist and toward your own well-being and goals, this will reduce the narcissist's influence in your life. This must be a sincere effort, of course, because narcissists are skilled at identifying deception. Actively invest time and energy into your own interests, friendships, and personal growth, so your partner does not consume your attention and emotional resources.

By building a rich and fulfilling life outside of your relationship, you send the message that you are not dependent on your partner for your sense of worth or happiness. This can be deeply unsettling for the narcissist, who thrives on being the center of attention and the most important person in your life.

2. Challenging the Narcissist's Idealized Self

Narcissists present to the world a grandiose, idealized version of themselves. This false self is often based on a deep sense of insecurity and shame, and they will go to great lengths to protect and defend this fragile ego structure.

One way to destabilize the narcissist's hold over you is to challenge this idealized self. This might involve pointing out inconsistencies in their stories, questioning their grandiose claims, or exposing the ways their actions don't align with their professed values. Take care to use this strategy with caution, however, and to ensure your own safety before instigating a confrontation. Narcissists can react with intense rage and aggression when their false self is threatened, so be sure to have a solid support system and exit strategy in place before challenging them directly.

3. Mapping and Challenging the False Self

In addition to challenging the narcissist's idealized self, it can also be effective to map out the specific elements of their false self and to identify areas where they are most vulnerable and insecure. This might mean paying close attention to the stories they tell about themselves, their accomplishments, or the qualities they claim to possess. Identifying the components of the narcissist's false self will help you see the cracks in their façade and understand the deep-seated fears and insecurities that drive their behavior.

Armed with this knowledge, you might begin to gently poke at these areas of vulnerability. This doesn't mean attacking them in a hostile way, but finding subtle ways to question or undermine their grandiose claims. For example, if they brag about their intelligence, you might casually mention a book or article that presents a different perspective on a topic they profess to be an expert in. Or if they pride themselves on their charm and social skills, you might point out a social faux pas or awkward interaction they had while in your presence.

The goal is not to humiliate or demean the narcissist, but rather to chip away at their façade and to force them to confront the reality of their own limitations and flaws.

4. Focusing on Your Own Healing and Growth

This means seeking therapy or counseling to process the trauma you have experienced as a result of your relationship, and developing healthy coping strategies and boundary-setting skills. It also means nurturing your own interests, passions, and relationships outside of your relationship. By building a life filled with joy, purpose, and authentic connection, you make it clear that you are not dependent on your partner for your sense of worth or happiness.

In many cases, the mere act of seeing their victim thriving and flourishing without them can be deeply unsettling for the narcissist. Often they will attempt to pull you back into the relationship or to sabotage your efforts at independence. If you can remain focused on your healing and growth, however, their efforts will fail, and your freedom will be in sight.

5. Disrupting the Narcissist's Supply

To maintain their sense of self, narcissists rely on a constant stream of admiration, attention, and validation from others. This "supply" is like a drug to them, and they will go to great lengths to secure it. But if you're able to cut off their supply, you could gain the upper hand. This might involve setting boundaries around your own emotional availability, refusing to engage in their attempts at triangulation or manipulation, or perhaps even exposing their true nature to others.

By denying the narcissist the validation and attention they crave, you can erode their sense of power and control. But again, while this can be a highly effective strategy, it's advised that you approach it with caution and have a support system in place. Narcissists can become highly agitated and sometimes even dangerous when they feel threatened, so prioritize your own safety and well-being above all else.

In some cases, permanently damaging the narcissist's supply may involve taking legal action, such as filing for divorce or seeking a restraining order. It may also mean reaching out to friends, family members, or colleagues to alert them about the narcissist's true nature and request their support in holding the narcissist accountable.

Naturally, much of this can be a difficult and painful process, but in some cases it's necessary in order to escape the grip of a narcissistic partner.

Other Techniques to Help Combat the Narcissist

1. The Red Herring Test: If you find yourself wondering if your partner is a narcissist, the red herring test can be a useful tool for gaining clarity. This involves intentionally revealing something emotionally compelling or vulnerable to your partner and noting how they respond over time.

In a healthy relationship, a loving partner would recognize the significance of your disclosure and would treat it with care and respect. They would not use it as a weapon or a means of manipulation.

A narcissist, on the other hand, will likely store this information away, waiting for the opportune moment to use it against you. They may bring it up during arguments, use it to shame or humiliate you, or reveal it to others as a way of discrediting or undermining you.

If you find that your partner repeatedly uses your vulnerabilities against you, it's a strong indication that you may be in a relationship with a narcissist.

2. Applying Occam's Razor: Occam's Razor is a philosophical principle which recommends that when faced with multiple hypotheses for something, one should choose the explanation that requires the fewest assumptions. When it comes to narcissistic behavior, applying this principle can help you discover the truth about your relationship.

If your partner consistently lies, cheats, or manipulates, the most logical explanation is that they are a narcissist who lacks empathy and concern for others. While it may be tempting to make excuses or to find more complex reasons for their behavior, applying Occam's Razor can help you see the situation more clearly and objectively.

3. The Grey Rock Technique: The grey rock technique is a strategy that involves making yourself as uninteresting and unremarkable as possible. The goal is to avoid providing the narcissist with any emotional reactions or personal information that they can use against you.

In practice, this means communicating in a very neutral, factual way and avoiding topics that could be emotionally charged or revealing. You might talk about the weather, current events, or practical matters, but steer clear of discussing your feelings, relationships, or personal struggles.

By presenting yourself as a "grey rock" - dull, unresponsive, and uninteresting - you deprive the narcissist of the attention and emotional reactions they crave. Over time, they may lose interest in you altogether, allowing you to create more distance and detachment in the relationship.

4. Strategies for Emotional Detachment: Other strategies you can use to emotionally detach from a narcissistic partner include:

- Focusing on your own needs, goals, and self-care

- Spending time with supportive friends and family members

- Engaging in activities and hobbies that bring you joy and fulfillment

- Practicing mindfulness and self-compassion

- Seeking therapy or counseling to process your emotions and develop coping strategies

By shifting your focus away from the narcissist and toward your own well-being, you can develop both emotional distance and perspective in your relationship.

5.   Combating Triangulation: As we've learned, triangulation is a manipulation tactic used by narcissists in which they bring a third party into the relationship dynamic to stoke jealousy, insecurity, or competition. To combat this tactic, insist on direct communication with your partner and avoid being drawn into their web of manipulation.

This might involve setting clear boundaries around your interactions with the third party, refusing to engage in gossip or comparison, and insisting on open, honest communication with your partner. Keeping the focus on your own relationship and communication can diffuse the power of the narcissist's triangulation attempts.

6.   Dealing with Flying Monkeys: "Flying monkeys" is a term used to describe the people who narcissists often recruit to do their bidding and to help them maintain control over their victims. These may be friends, family members, or even professionals who have been manipulated into taking the narcissist's side and undermining the victim's perception of reality.

To deal with flying monkeys, have a plan in place before they strike. This might involve:

- Setting clear boundaries with the flying monkeys and refusing to engage in discussions about the narcissist

- Seeking support from trusted friends, family members, or professionals who can provide a reality check and validation

- Keeping records of abusive or manipulative behavior to counter any false narratives spread by the flying monkeys

- Limiting or cutting off all contact with the flying monkeys if necessary

Anticipating the narcissist's use of these people and having a plan to deal with them can minimize their impact and help you maintain your peace of mind.

7. Developing Planned Responses: One of the most effective ways to combat narcissistic manipulation is to have planned responses on hand whenever the narcissist attempts to gaslight, shame, or blame you. This means:

- Practicing assertive communication techniques, such as using "I" statements and setting clear boundaries

- Developing scripts or mantras that you can use to counter the narcissist's manipulation (e.g. "I know what I experienced," "I am not responsible for your emotions")

- Roleplaying scenarios with a therapist or trusted friend to practice responding effectively to the narcissist's tactics

Having responses at the read can help you feel empowered and in control when your partner attempts to manipulate you.

8. Other Techniques for Disarming Narcissists: While the goal of combating narcissistic abuse is not to seek revenge or to "win" the relationship, there are some techniques that can be effective in frustrating the narcissist and exposing their true nature. These might include:

- Refusing to engage in arguments or power struggles, and instead disengaging or walking away

- Using humor or sarcasm to deflect the narcissist's attempts at control or manipulation

- Exposing the narcissist's behavior to others in a calm, factual way

- Focusing on your own success, happiness, and well-being, and refusing to let the narcissist's opinion of you define your self-worth

Employing these techniques strategically and perhaps even with the guidance of a trained professional will help you shift the power dynamic in your relationship and assert your individuality and identity.

As we've explored throughout this chapter, combating narcissistic manipulation requires a combination of self-awareness, emotional detachment, and strategic communication. But it's important to remember that these techniques are not a long-term solution to the problem of narcissistic abuse. While they can help you cope with the day-to-day challenges of your relationship, the ultimate goal should be to free yourself from their hold on you.

In many cases, this means making the difficult decision to leave the relationship and forge a new life for yourself. While this can be a daunting and painful process, it is often the only way to truly free yourself from the toxicity of a relationship with a narcissist.

In the next chapter, we'll explore ways to safely and effectively leave a narcissistic relationship. We'll discuss the challenges that can arise, and provide practical strategies for navigating this difficult transition with courage, clarity, and self-compassion.

Chapter 7: Exiting a Narcissistic Relationship for Good

"The most courageous act is still to think for yourself. Aloud." - Coco Chanel

The decision to leave a narcissistic relationship can be quite difficult, but it's also a courageous step toward a healthier life. It's a journey fraught with emotional turmoil and self-doubt. In this chapter, we'll explore the process of exiting a relationship with a narcissist, focusing on the emotional and practical aspects of this significant life change.

Before we delve into the details, it's important to note that while some narcissists may exhibit *physically* abusive behavior, most do not. This chapter focuses on the more common emotional and psychological aspects of leaving a narcissistic relationship. If you are in a physically abusive situation, please seek immediate help from domestic violence resources in your area.

Emma's Story: A Quiet Departure

Emma, a 34-year-old graphic designer, had been with Robert for five years. From the outside, their relationship seemed perfect. Robert was charming, successful, and always the life of the party. But behind closed doors, Emma felt like she was disappearing.

Robert's criticism was constant but subtle. He'd make offhand comments about her work, her appearance, even her friends and family. He'd dismiss her accomplishments, implying they weren't that big a deal. When Emma expressed feelings of discontent with his

words or behaviors, Robert would accuse her of being "too sensitive" or "misunderstanding" his intentions.

Over time, Emma found herself second-guessing her decisions. She stopped sharing her successes at work, knowing Robert would find a way to diminish them. Her friendships dwindled as she withdrew, afraid of Robert's judgmental comments about her social life.

It wasn't until Emma started therapy for her growing anxiety that she began to recognize the patterns of narcissistic behavior in her relationship. With her therapist's help, she started to see how Robert's behavior - the subtle put-downs, the gaslighting, the way he always turned conversations back to himself - aligned with narcissistic traits.

The decision to leave didn't come easily. Emma feared being alone, starting over in her late-30s, and facing the disbelief of friends who saw Robert as the perfect partner. But she also recognized that staying meant continuing to shrink herself and live with constant anxiety.

Emma's process of leaving was quiet but deliberate. She focused on rebuilding her sense of self, reconnecting with old friends, and slowly creating a life independent of Robert. When she finally told him she was leaving, she was prepared for his attempts at manipulation - the guilt trips, the promises to change, the subtle threats about how she'd never find anyone better.

Emma's story illustrates the difficulties of leaving a narcissistic relationship. It's rarely a single, dramatic moment, but rather a series of small steps and realizations that lead to the final decision to leave.

In this chapter, we'll explore the various stages of exiting a narcissistic relationship, from recognizing it's time to leave, to planning your departure, to handling the immediate aftermath. We'll discuss strategies for maintaining your resolve in the face of manipulation tactics, and provide guidance on navigating the practical aspects of separation.

Remember, leaving a narcissist is not just about physically removing yourself from the relationship - it's about reclaiming your sense of self, your autonomy, and your right to a healthy, fulfilling life.

Recognizing When It's Time to Leave

Deciding to leave a narcissistic relationship is rarely a sudden or easy decision. Often, it's the culmination of numerous small realizations and a gradual understanding that the relationship is harmful to your well-being. Here are some signs that it may be time to consider leaving:

1. Persistent Feelings of Inadequacy: If you constantly feel like you're not good enough, despite your best efforts, it may be due to the narcissist's continuous criticism and devaluation.

2. Walking on Eggshells: Feeling like you need to constantly monitor your behavior to avoid upsetting your partner is a sign of an unhealthy dynamic.

3. Gaslighting: If your partner frequently contradicts your perceptions and memories, you may be experiencing gaslighting.

4. Loss of Self: Realizing that you've given up hobbies, friendships, or aspects of your personality to please your partner is a red flag.

5. Emotional Exhaustion: Feeling constantly drained from managing your partner's emotions and needs at the expense of your own is unsustainable.

6. Lack of Empathy: If your partner consistently fails to

understand or care about your feelings, it's a clear sign of narcissistic behavior.

7. Cyclical Arguments: Conflicts between you never truly resolve, but instead cycle through the same patterns without real change.

Emotional Preparation for Leaving

Once you've recognized that it's time to leave, emotional preparation is crucial. This process may take time. Here are some steps to consider:

1. Validate Your Experience: Acknowledge that your feelings are real and valid. Narcissists often make their partners doubt their own perceptions, so affirming your experience is an important first step.

2. Build a Support System: Confide in friends, family members, or even a therapist. Having support is beneficial during this difficult time.

3. Reconnect with Your Identity: Start rediscovering who you are outside of the relationship. Revisit old hobbies or interests that you may have neglected.

4. Set Small Goals: Begin with small, achievable goals that are just for you. This can help rebuild your confidence and sense of autonomy.

5. Educate Yourself: Learn more about NPD and the effects of narcissistic abuse. Understanding the dynamics at play can help you make sense of your experience.

6. Practice Self-Compassion: Be kind to yourself. Recognize that you've been in a difficult situation and that healing takes time.

7. Envision Your Future: Start imagining what your life could look like without your narcissistic partner.

8. Prepare for Guilt and Doubt: Understand that feelings of guilt or doubt about leaving are normal. These feelings don't mean you should stay.

Remember, emotional preparation is not a single event. It's okay to take your time and move at a pace that feels right for you. The goal is to strengthen your resolve and build the emotional resilience you'll need to make the break and begin healing.

Planning Your Departure

Once you've made the decision to leave and have begun your emotional preparation, it's time to consider the practical aspects of your departure. Here are some key steps to consider:

1. Financial Planning:

    o   Open a separate bank account if you don't already have one.

    o   Start setting aside money if possible.

    o   Gather important financial documents (bank statements, tax returns, etc.).

    o   If you share accounts or debts, consult with a financial advisor or lawyer about the best way to proceed.

2. Living Arrangements:

    o   If you're living together, start quietly looking for a new place to live.

    o   If you own property together, consult with a lawyer about your options.

o   Prepare an exit strategy that ensures your safety and privacy.

3.   Personal Belongings:

o   Be sure you've collected those personal items and documents that are valuable to you.

4.   Support Network:

o   Consider consulting friends or family members about your plans and getting their feedback.

5.   Professional Support:

o   Consider engaging a therapist who specializes in narcissistic abuse recovery.

o   If legal issues are involved, consult with a lawyer.

6.   Digital Security:

o   Change passwords on all personal accounts.

o   Create new email addresses if necessary.

o   Review privacy settings on social media accounts.

Handling the Conversation

Informing a narcissistic partner about your decision to leave requires careful consideration. Here are some strategies to keep in mind:

1.   Choose the Right Time and Place:

o   Select a time when you won't be interrupted.

o   Choose a neutral location if you're concerned about their reaction.

2. Be Clear and Firm:

   o State your decision clearly and directly.

   o Leave no room for ambiguity or false hope.

   o Use "I" statements to express your feelings and decisions.

3. Prepare for Various Reactions:

   o Narcissists may react with anger, guilt-tripping, promises to change, or attempts to manipulate you into staying.

   o Stay calm and stick to your decision, regardless of their reaction.

4. Avoid Lengthy Explanations:

   o You don't necessarily owe the narcissist a detailed explanation of your reasons for leaving, so try to keep your conversation brief and to the point.

5. Set Clear Boundaries:

   o Establish clear boundaries about future contact.

   o Be prepared to enforce these boundaries consistently.

Example Script: "[Partner's name], this isn't working for me anymore and I'm leaving. I've told you many times how unhappy I am, but you haven't listened and now I need to move on. I understand this is difficult to hear, but my decision is final. I'd appreciate it if you could respect my choice and my need for space during this transition."

Remember, your safety and well-being are paramount. If at any point you feel unsafe or overwhelmed, it's okay to leave the situation immediately. Trust your instincts and prioritize your own needs.

Navigating the Immediate Aftermath

The period immediately following your departure from a narcissistic relationship can be emotionally turbulent. Here's how to navigate this rocky time:

1. Anticipating and Handling Manipulation Tactics

Narcissists often employ various strategies to regain control or punish you for leaving. Being prepared can help you resist these tactics:

a) Hoovering:

- The narcissist may attempt to "suck you back in" with grand gestures, promises of change, or displays of remorse.

- Stay firm in your decision. Remember why you left and that genuine change is extremely rare in a narcissist.

b) Guilt-tripping:

- They might try to make you feel responsible for their well-being or the relationship's failure.

- Remind yourself that you're not responsible for their emotions or actions.

c) Rage and Intimidation:

- Some narcissists may react with anger or threats when their control is threatened.

- Prioritize your safety. Don't hesitate to involve law enforcement if you feel threatened.

d) Smear Campaigns:

- The narcissist might spread false information about you to mutual friends, family, or colleagues.

- Resist the urge to defend yourself publicly. Those who truly know you will see through the lies.

e) Silent Treatment:

- Some narcissists may attempt to punish you by cutting off all communication.

- While painful, this can actually aid in your healing process. Use this time to focus on yourself.

2. Managing Your Emotional Response

Leaving a narcissistic relationship can trigger a range of intense emotions. Here's how to cope:

a) Allow Yourself to Grieve:

- It's normal to mourn the end of a relationship, even if it was toxic.

- Give yourself permission to feel sadness, anger, relief, or any other emotions that arise.

b) Practice Self-Care:

- Prioritize your physical and emotional well-being.

- Engage in activities that bring you comfort and joy.

c) Resist the Urge to Make Contact:

- You may feel tempted to reach out to your ex-partner, especially if you're feeling lonely.

- Remind yourself why you left and stay committed to your decision.

d) Seek Support:

- Lean on friends and family.

- Consider joining a support group.

e) Be Patient with Yourself:

- Healing is not linear. You will probably have good days and bad days.

- Be kind to yourself throughout the process.

3. Practical Considerations

a) Communication Boundaries:

- Consider implementing a "no contact" rule if you feel it will help you move on.

- If communication is necessary (e.g., co-parenting), keep it brief and business-like.

b) Social Media:

- Consider blocking or unfollowing your ex on all platforms.

- Be cautious about what you post, as narcissists often monitor their ex-partners' social media.

c) Mutual Friends:

- Be prepared for some friends to take sides or distance themselves.

- Focus on nurturing relationships with those who support your decision.

d) Legal and Financial Matters:

- If you were married or have shared assets, consult with a lawyer about next steps.

- Be vigilant about your finances and credit, as your ex may attempt financial retaliation.

Maintaining Resolve and Beginning the Healing Process

The weeks and months following your departure from a narcissistic relationship can be a rollercoaster of emotions. While you've taken the healthy step of leaving, the road ahead requires ongoing commitment and self-compassion.

One of the greatest hurdles you may face is the temptation to return to the relationship. The familiar, even if toxic, can sometimes feel more comfortable than the unknown. You might find yourself remembering only the good times, or doubting your decision during moments of loneliness. This is a normal part of the process, but stay firm in your resolve.

To help maintain your commitment to your new life, consider creating a "reminder list" - a document where you record the reasons you left and the negative aspects of the relationship. Review this list whenever you feel your resolve wavering. This tangible reminder can help ground you in your decision and reinforce your commitment to your well-being.

As you move through this new chapter in your life, you may encounter what therapists often call "emotional flashbacks" - sudden, intense feelings of worthlessness, shame, or anxiety that harken back to your experiences in the narcissistic relationship. These flashbacks can be disorienting and painful, but they're a normal part of the healing process. When they occur, try to ground yourself in the present moment. Remind yourself that these feelings, while intense, will pass.

Building a new support network can be extremely helpful during this time. Some of your old friendships may have been strained or lost during the relationship, and you might feel isolated. Don't be afraid to reach out and reconnect with old friends, or to seek out new connections. Support groups can be particularly helpful, offering understanding and validation from others who have had similar experiences.

As you begin to recover, you might notice changes in yourself. Many survivors of narcissistic relationships find themselves becoming more assertive, setting clearer boundaries, and valuing their own needs and desires more highly than they used to. Embrace these changes - they're signs of growth and positivity.

Remember, while you might have days where you feel strong and empowered, these might be followed by days where you feel lost or unsure of yourself. This ebb and flow is normal. Be patient and remind yourself that healing is a journey, not a destination.

In time, you will likely find yourself ready to consider new relationships. It's important to move at your own pace and not rush this process. Take time to rediscover yourself, your likes and dislikes, your goals and dreams. As you do, you'll be better equipped to recognize healthy relationship dynamics and to develop new connections from a place of strength and self-awareness.

The end of your narcissistic relationship marks the beginning of a new chapter in your life - one where you are the author of your own story. While the journey can be difficult, it also holds the promise of freedom, authenticity, and the opportunity to create a life that truly reflects your values and desires.

In our next and final chapter, we'll explore the long-term healing process. We'll learn strategies for rebuilding self-esteem, processing trauma, and creating a fulfilling life beyond narcissistic abuse.

Chapter 8:
Healing from Narcissist Abuse and Moving Forward

Sarah had finally found the courage to leave her narcissistic partner after years of emotional and psychological abuse. As she sat in her new apartment, surrounded by boxes and the remnants of her old life, she felt a mix of relief, exhaustion, and uncertainty. She knew that leaving had been the right decision, but the road ahead seemed daunting.

Conflicting emotions swirled within her. On one hand, her new apartment was a space that was entirely her own, free from the constant tension that had characterized her life with her ex-partner. She could breathe easier here, without the weight of his judgment, criticism, and control spotlighting her every move.

On the other hand, the apartment also felt strangely empty, a stark reminder of all she had left behind. The photographs on the walls, the books on the shelves, the mementos and trinkets that had once held such meaning - all of these things felt like relics from a life that she had shed like a snake shedding its skin.

As Sarah began to unpack her boxes and settle into her new surroundings, she found herself grappling with a profound sense of loss and disorientation. For so long, her identity had been tied to her relationship with her ex-partner, shaped and molded by his manipulation. She had lost touch with her own desires, dreams, and sense of self.

In the early days and weeks after leaving, Sarah often found herself questioning her decision, wondering if she had made a terrible mistake. The trauma bond that had kept her tethered to her ex-partner was still strong, and she found herself longing for the familiarity and security of the relationship, even as she knew that it had been poisonous and destructive.

Perhaps you've taken the same path as Sarah and are now grappling with these same questions. The purpose of this book is to guide you through the process of understanding narcissism, recognizing the signs of abuse, and ultimately breaking free from the narcissist's grip, so now it's time to focus on healing and moving forward.

Recovery from narcissistic abuse may not always be easy, but you are not alone. There are countless others who have walked this path before you and have found healing and renewal on the other side. This chapter will provide you with the tools, strategies, and support you need to cope with the aftermath of narcissistic abuse, so that you may reclaim your agency and build a life of joy and fulfillment.

Coping with the Aftermath of Narcissistic Abuse

Emotional healing and recovery

Leaving a relationship with a narcissist is only the beginning of the healing process. You may find yourself grappling with a range of intense emotions once you're out, including grief, anger, shame, and confusion. These feelings are normal and valid, so give yourself permission to fully experience and process them.

Part of emotional healing is learning to practice self-compassion. You may find yourself engaging in self-blame or self-criticism, wondering how you could have allowed yourself to become involved with a narcissist in the first place. This is when you must remind yourself that none of it was your fault and that you lacked the information and resources you needed to make an informed choice about your future.

Seeking support: therapy, support groups, and resources

Healing from narcissistic abuse is not a journey you have to undertake alone. Seeking support from trained professionals and fellow survivors can be a crucial component of your recovery process. A therapist who specializes in narcissistic abuse recovery can provide you with a safe and non-judgmental space to process your experiences, develop coping strategies, and work through any lingering trauma or self-doubt.

Support groups, whether in-person or online, can also be a valuable resource. Connecting with others who have experienced similar struggles can help you feel less alone and provide you with a sense of validation and understanding. Many survivors find that sharing their stories and hearing about the experiences of others can be a powerful source of healing and empowerment.

Rebuilding self-esteem and self-worth

One of the most insidious effects of narcissistic abuse is the way it can erode one's sense of self-worth and self-esteem. After years of being told that you are not good enough, that your feelings and needs don't matter, and that you are lucky to have the narcissist in your life, it can be tough to rebuild a strong and healthy sense of self.

The process often begins with learning to set boundaries and prioritize your own needs and well-being. Practice saying no to unreasonable requests, carving out time for self-care and relaxation, and surrounding yourself with supportive and affirming relationships.

Additionally, it is often beneficial to engage in activities that promote a sense of mastery and accomplishment, like learning a new skill, taking on a challenging project at work, or pursuing a long-held dream. By proving to yourself that you are capable and deserving of success and happiness, you can chip away at the negative self-image that your ex instilled in you.

Learn to forgive yourself, but not the narcissist

As you move down the path of healing, you may find yourself grappling with the question of forgiveness. But forgiveness is a deeply personal process and there is no one-size-fits-all approach.

For many, the idea of forgiving the narcissist can feel impossible or even detrimental to their well-being. After all, the narcissist's actions were not accidental or misguided, but likely a deliberate pattern of manipulation and control. Holding them accountable for their behavior and refusing to absolve them of responsibility can be a critical part of the healing process.

However, it is crucial to distinguish between forgiving the narcissist and forgiving yourself. Many survivors find themselves struggling with feelings of guilt, shame, and self-blame after they've left the relationship. Learning to forgive yourself for any mistakes or weaknesses will aid the healing process.

Engage in things like contradicting negative self-talk, practicing self-compassion, and reminding yourself that you did the best you could under the circumstances. Release yourself from the burden of self-blame and shame.

Empowering Yourself and Reclaiming Your Life

Reclaiming your agency and autonomy

After years of being involved with a narcissist, you may find yourself struggling to trust your own instincts and make decisions for yourself.

Reclaiming your agency often begins with small, everyday choices, like deciding what to wear, what to eat, or how to spend your free time without seeking the approval or permission of another. As you become more comfortable making these small decisions, you can work towards larger decisions, like setting career goals, pursuing new relationships, or making major life changes.

It's also a good idea to practice assertiveness and boundary-setting in your interactions with others. In other words, learn to express your needs and opinions clearly and confidently, even in the face of pushback or resistance. Standing up for yourself and your values will help you rebuild a sense of self-respect and self-worth.

Addressing people-pleasing tendencies

Many survivors of narcissistic abuse realize they have people-pleasing tendencies. After years of being conditioned to prioritize someone else's needs and desires above their own, it can be difficult to break yourself of this pattern of self-sacrifice.

If this describes you, learn to recognize and question the underlying beliefs and fears that drive this behavior. Perhaps you have a fear of rejection, abandonment, or conflict, or a deep-seated belief that your worth is contingent upon the approval and acceptance of others.

If you can learn to validate your own needs, set healthy boundaries, and be prepared to disappoint others now and then, you're on the path to a more authentic and self-directed way of relating to others.

Rediscovering personal interests and passions

Narcissistic relationships often involve a gradual erosion of the victim's sense of self and individuality. As the narcissist demands more and more of your time, energy, and attention, you may find yourself losing touch with the activities, hobbies, and passions that once brought you joy and fulfillment.

Rediscovering your personal interests and passions is an important component of healing. Consider revisiting old hobbies or pursuits that you abandoned during the relationship, or exploring new activities and experiences that spark your curiosity and enthusiasm.

Reconnecting with your authentic desires and passions will encourage you to rebuild a sense of identity and purpose in life.

Establishing new, healthy relationships

Establishing new, healthy relationships is a valuable step in the healing process. After experiencing the toxicity of a narcissistic relationship, you may have trouble trusting others and opening yourself up to new connections.

You'll be happy to hear that there's no need to rush into anything. Take things slowly and prioritize your own well-being, which may involve setting boundaries around your time and emotional energy, being selective about the people you allow into your life, and learning to communicate assertively about your needs and expectations.

You might find it useful to learn more about the qualities of healthy, mutually supportive relationships, such as respect, empathy, honesty, and a willingness to compromise and work through conflicts in a constructive way. By surrounding yourself with people who embody these qualities and who support and affirm your own growth and healing, you can rebuild feelings of trust and connection in your relationships.

Understanding that healing takes time

Healing from narcissistic abuse is a process that requires patience, self-compassion, and a willingness to sit with difficult emotions. There is no set timeline for recovery and each person's journey will be unique to them. Give yourself permission to process your experiences on your own time, as you develop new coping strategies and rebuild your sense of self.

Educating yourself about narcissism

Educating yourself about NPD and the dynamics of narcissistic abuse can be truly empowering. It can help you make sense of your experiences and develop a greater understanding of what you've been through. This knowledge can also help you recognize and protect yourself from narcissists in the future.

Accepting that the narcissist will not change

Recognizing the reality that a narcissist is unlikely to change their behavior or take responsibility for their actions can be a turning point for a victim. Narcissists are often deeply invested in maintaining their false self-image and sense of superiority, and are likely to resist attempts to hold them accountable or that encourage them to seek help. By accepting this, you can begin to let go of any lingering hopes or expectations for the relationship and focus on your own growth and forward movement.

Seeking professional help

Seeking the guidance and support of a mental health professional who specializes in narcissistic abuse recovery can be an invaluable step in the healing process. A therapist can provide you with a safe and non-judgmental space to share your experiences, work through any trauma or self-doubt, and develop coping strategies and communication skills. They can also help you navigate legal or practical challenges that may arise as you disentangle yourself from your former partner.

Recognizing enablers (flying monkeys) in the narcissist's life

As we discussed earlier, narcissists often surround themselves with enablers who support and reinforce their manipulative behavior. These "flying monkeys" may be friends, family members, or even professionals who have been fooled by the narcissist's charming façade and who may unwittingly participate in the abuse by taking the narcissist's side or minimizing the victim's experiences. Learning to recognize and set boundaries with these people will help you protect yourself from further manipulation.

Recognizing your role and seeking allies

In the aftermath of a narcissistic relationship, it's advisable to take an honest look at any patterns or tendencies that may have made you vulnerable to a narcissist in the first place. Perhaps you have a history of trauma, codependency, or people-pleasing behavior. By recognizing these patterns and addressing them with the help of a therapist or support group, you will be able to develop healthier relationships in the future. You should also seek out allies and other supportive people who can provide validation, encouragement, and a sense of community as you heal.

Setting boundaries and getting attuned with your feelings and body

The ability to set and maintain healthy boundaries means learning to say no to unreasonable requests, prioritizing your own needs, and communicating your limits clearly and assertively. Become attuned with your own feelings and bodily sensations, as these can provide valuable information about your needs and boundaries. Listen to and trust your own inner wisdom, so you can develop a stronger sense of self and a greater capacity for self-care and self-protection.

Recognizing triggers and replacing them with empowering activities

The healing process often involves learning to recognize and manage emotional triggers - situations, people, or experiences that evoke painful memories or feelings related to the abuse you suffered. By developing an awareness of your triggers and learning to respond to them in healthy ways, you can break free from the hold of a narcissist. Consider replacing triggering activities or relationships with more positive and affirming ones, such as spending time in nature, engaging in creative pursuits, or connecting with friends and family members.

Stopping self-blame and self-destructive behaviors

Narcissistic abuse often leaves victims struggling with feelings of shame, self-blame, and worthlessness. These negative beliefs can lead to self-destructive behaviors like substance abuse, self-harm, or staying in toxic relationships. It's vital for your mental health to learn to challenge these negative beliefs and replace them with more accurate and compassionate ones. Consider working with a therapist to develop new self-talk and coping strategies, and make an effort to surround yourself with positive and affirming messages and relationships.

Embracing self-care, breathing techniques, and meditation

Self-care during the healing process will help reduce stress, promote relaxation, and support overall physical and emotional well-being. You might think about engaging in practices such as deep breathing, meditation, yoga, or other mindfulness techniques that can help to calm the nervous system and promote a sense of inner peace and clarity. It's also important to prioritize basic self-care activities like getting enough sleep, eating a healthy diet, and engaging in regular exercise and social connection.

Reclaiming your laughter and listening to your instincts

Narcissistic abuse can often rob victims of their sense of joy, spontaneity, and inner wisdom. Learning to reclaim these qualities and trust in your own instincts and desires will vastly improve your recovery. FInd activities and relationships that bring you genuine happiness and fulfillment, and try to listen to and act on your own inner guidance, even when it goes against what others may be telling you.

Listing your accomplishments and releasing shame

Developing a practice of regularly acknowledging and celebrating your own strengths, accomplishments, and positive qualities can counteract the feelings of self-doubt that can linger after a relationship with a narcissist. Doing things like keeping a journal of your successes and milestones, sharing your achievements with supportive friends and family members, or working with a therapist to develop a more accurate and compassionate view of yourself are valuable additions to your arsenal of tools to help you move past your relationship.

Learning to let go and understanding key affirmations

Letting go of the pain, anger, and attachment that often follow a relationship with a narcissist is a gradual and ongoing process. It requires a willingness to feel and process difficult emotions, as well as a commitment to focusing on your own growth rather than trying to change or control your ex-partner. Some affirmations that can support the process include:

- "I am not responsible for the narcissist's behavior or happiness."

- "I deserve to be treated with respect and kindness."

- "I trust my own perceptions and experiences."

- "I am capable of creating a happy and fulfilling life without the narcissist."

- "I release the need for the narcissist's approval or validation."

If you regularly repeat these affirmations and surround yourself with supportive messages and relationships, you'll gradually find yourself feeling stronger and more able to move on with a fulfilling and self-directed life without the interference of a narcissist.

Fully Recovering from a Narcissistic Relationship

Understanding co-idealization and the narcissist's influence on your mind

After you've left a toxic relationship with a narcissist, it's common to struggle with a phenomenon known as "co-idealization" - a process in which both the narcissist and their victim become emotionally and psychologically enmeshed, each projecting idealized qualities onto the other. This can lead to feelings of confusion and disorientation when the relationship ends, as the victim may struggle to separate their own identity and reality from that of the narcissist. Understanding and disentangling from this concept is part of the healing journey.

Coping with feelings of guilt, anxiety, and "abandoning" the narcissist

After leaving a narcissistic relationship, many victims struggle with guilt, anxiety, and the feeling they've "abandoned" the narcissist. These feelings are often the result of the narcissist's manipulations, which can leave victims feeling responsible for the narcissist's happiness and well-being, even at the expense of their own. It can be valuable to work with a therapist or support group who can help you identify and challenge these distorted beliefs, so you can dispel them and move on with yoru life.

Re-individuating and detaching from the narcissist's reality

"Re-individuation" is the process of separating oneself from the narcissist's reality and reclaiming one's own identity, values, and beliefs. This can be a painful process, as it often involves confronting the ways in which the narcissist's influence has infiltrated your mind and sense of self. However, by gradually detaching from their worldview and learning to trust your own perceptions and experiences, you will find that you are stronger and can develop a more authentic sense of self.

Steps to fully recover

1. Break the habit of projecting moral values onto the narcissist: Recognize that narcissists operate according to their own self-serving moral code, and that it's futile to expect them to adhere to the same ethical standards as non-narcissists.

2. Validate your own reality: Learn to trust your own perceptions, memories, and experiences, even when they conflict with the narcissist's version of events.

3. Create a solid support network: Surround yourself with people who believe you, support you, and encourage you to prioritize your own needs and well-being.

4. Maintain no/low contact with the narcissist: Establish clear boundaries around communication and interaction with your ex, in order to protect yourself from further manipulation.

5. Reconnect with your pre-narcissist identity: Rediscover the interests, values, and relationships that were important to you before your toxic relationship and work to reintegrate these into your post-narcissist life.

6. Reframe the experience to benefit your mental state: Look for ways to find meaning, growth, or purpose in your experience, rather than allowing your former relationship to define you or hold you back.

7. Replace cravings to reconnect with the narcissist with healthier connections and activities: When the urge to reach out to your ex arises, redirect your energy toward self-care, supportive relationships, or meaningful pursuits.

8. Engage in self-care: Prioritize activities that promote your physical, emotional, and spiritual well-being, such as exercise, creative expression, time in nature, and social connection.

Working through these steps and surrounding yourself with support and resources will speed your recovery from the trauma of narcissistic abuse and lead you to build a life of greater peace, authenticity, and fulfillment. Remind yourself that healing is a journey, not a destination - be patient, celebrate your progress, and trust in your own resilience.

Resources for Further Support

Books, articles, and websites

There are many valuable resources available for those seeking to deepen their understanding of narcissistic abuse and support their healing journey. Below is a list of some recommended books:

- *Psychopath Free* by Jackson MacKenzie

- *Why Does He Do That?* by Lundy Bancroft

- *Should I Stay or Should I Go?* by Ramani Durvasula

- *The Covert Passive-Aggressive Narcissist* by Debbie Mirza

- *Healing from Hidden Abuse* by Shannon Thomas

In addition to books, there are countless articles and websites that offer insights and strategies for recovery from narcissistic abuse. Some recommended online resources include:

- PsychCentral.com

- TheHotline.org

- NarcissisticAbuseSupport.com

- OutoftheStorm.website

- HealingFromComplexTraumaAndPTSD.com

Online communities and support groups

Connecting with others who have experienced narcissistic abuse can be a great source of validation, support, and encouragement. Some recommended online communities and support groups include:

- Reddit.com/r/NarcissisticAbuse

- Reddit.com/r/NarcissisticSpouses

- Reddit.com/r/LifeAfterNarcissism

- SupportGroups.com

- ThePurpleLily.com

- Facebook.com/groups/NarcissisticVictimsExperiencedAbuse

These communities offer a safe and non-judgmental space to share experiences, ask for advice, and connect with others who understand the unique challenges involved in extricating oneself from the clutches of a narcissist.

Finding therapists and counselors specializing in narcissistic abuse

Working with a therapist or counselor who specializes in narcissistic abuse recovery can be an invaluable part of the healing process. To find a qualified professional in your area, the following resources can help:

- PsychologyToday.com

- GoodTherapy.org

- TherapyRoute.com

- TheNationalDomesticViolenceHotline.org

- Your local domestic violence agency or women's shelter

When searching for a therapist, consider finding someone who has experience working with survivors of narcissistic abuse and who uses evidence-based treatments such as cognitive-behavioral therapy (CBT), trauma-focused therapy, or eye movement desensitization and reprocessing (EMDR).

The most important thing to remember is that healing is not a linear process. You will likely experience setbacks and challenges along the way. But if you can remain committed to your own well-being, surround yourself with support and resources, and practice self-compassion and patience, you will forge a new life as a stronger, wiser, and more empowered you!

Conclusion

Sarah sat on the beach, her toes digging into the warm sand as she watched the sun dip below the horizon. The sky was painted in a stunning array of oranges, pinks, and purples, a breathtaking reminder of the beauty of the natural world.

As she sat there, Sarah reflected on her journey of resilience and transformation. Just a year ago, she had been trapped in a relationship with a narcissistic partner, a man who had slowly eroded her sense of self and left her feeling small and worthless. She had spent years walking on eggshells, trying to anticipate his moods and avoid his anger and sarcasm, convincing herself that if she just loved him enough, he would change.

But he never did change. Instead, Sarah reached a breaking point where she realized that she could no longer sacrifice her own well-being for the sake of a toxic relationship. With the help of a therapist, supportive friends, and her own inner strength, she found the courage to leave her narcissistic partner and begin the process of healing.

At first, Sarah was overwhelmed by the intensity of her emotions. She struggled with self-doubt and lingering feelings of attachment to her ex-partner, even though she realized the relationship had been unhealthy and abusive. But slowly, day by day, she began to rediscover her own voice, her own desires, and her own sense of self.

She learned more about NPD and the dynamics of narcissistic abuse. She read books, joined support groups, and worked with a therapist who specialized in helping victims of toxic relationships. Through this process, she discovered that her experiences were not unique, and that she was not to blame for her ex-partner's behavior.

Sarah also learned to set boundaries and prioritize her own needs and well-being. She learned to say no to requests that she knew would drain her energy or violate her values, and she surrounded herself with people who treated her with respect and kindness. She rediscovered hobbies and passions that she had neglected during her relationship, and she found joy in simple pleasures like walks in nature, cooking delicious meals, and having heartfelt conversations with friends.

Sarah began to reframe her experiences in a way that empowered her and gave her a sense of purpose. She started volunteering at a local animal shelter, took up art classes, and even began writing a blog about her experience, hoping to inspire others who were struggling with similar challenges.

As she sat there on the sand, Sarah realized that her journey was far from over. Healing from a toxic relationship was not a destination, but an ongoing process of growth, self-discovery, and transformation. She knew there would be setbacks along the way, but she also knew that she had the tools, the support, and the inner strength to face them.

As the last rays of sunlight disappeared behind the horizon, Sarah took a deep breath and whispered to herself: "I am worthy of love, respect, and happiness, and I will never again settle for anything less."

Sarah's story is a testament to all those who have endured narcissistic abuse and decided to leave. Her story illustrates the lessons and strategies that we have explored throughout this book – the importance of education and self-awareness, the power of boundaries and self-care, the value of reframing experiences and finding purpose in life after detaching from a narcissist.

As we near the end of this book, I want to leave you with a few points that I hope you will carry with you as you continue on your path to healing and freedom:

1. This was not your fault. No matter what your narcissistic partner may have told you, you are not to blame for their abusive behavior. Narcissists are skilled manipulators who know how to twist reality and make their victims feel responsible for their own mistreatment. But the truth is, no one deserves to be abused, and you are not responsible for your partner's choices or actions.

2. There's no need to forgive a narcissist, but you must forgive yourself. Holding onto anger and resentment toward your ex will only keep you trapped in the past and prevent you from moving forward. Focus on forgiving yourself for any perceived mistakes or weaknesses, and release yourself from the burden of blame and shame.

3. You can have a better life. Your experiences in a narcissistic relationship do not define you, and they do not limit your potential for happiness and fulfillment. By working through the healing process and surrounding yourself with support and positivity, you can create a life that is rich, meaningful, and full of joy.

4. You do deserve better. No matter what your narcissistic partner may have told you, you are worthy of love, respect, and kindness. You deserve to be treated with compassion, empathy, and understanding, and you have the right to set boundaries and advocate for your own needs and well-being.

Key Takeaways

Throughout this book, we have explored the complex dynamics of narcissistic relationships and the strategies for breaking free and healing from narcissistic abuse. Let's take a moment to recap some of the key takeaways from each chapter:

- Chapter 1: Understanding Narcissism: We explored the characteristics and behaviors of narcissistic personality disorder, the spectrum of narcissism and the ways in which narcissists manipulate and control their victims.

- Chapter 2: Recognizing Narcissistic Patterns in Relationships: We examined the common patterns and red flags of narcissistic relationships, including love bombing, gaslighting, and the cycle of idealization, devaluation, and discarding.

- Chapter 3: The Impact of Narcissism on Partners: We discussed the profound emotional, psychological, and physical effects of narcissistic abuse on victims, and the value of support and validation in the healing process.

- Chapter 4: Relationship Self-Assessment Guide: In this chapter is a comprehensive self-assessment tool to help you evaluate the health/toxicity of your relationship, and gain clarity on the signs of narcissistic abuse.

- Chapter 5: Breaking Free from Narcissistic Influence: We learned about strategies for detaching emotionally from a narcissistic partner, setting boundaries, and reclaiming one's autonomy and sense of self.

- Chapter 6: Techniques to End the Gaslighting and Manipulative Tactics: We talked about specific techniques for combating narcissistic manipulation, including the gray rock method, documentation, and seeking legal and professional support.

- Chapter 7: Exiting the Narcissistic Relationship for Good: This chapter provides a step-by-step guide for safely and effectively leaving a toxic relationship, including strategies for self-care, building a support network, and navigating the legal and practical challenges of the process.

- Chapter 8: Healing from Narcissist Abuse and Moving Forward: Finally, we discussed the journey of healing and recovery from a narcissistic relationship, including strategies for processing trauma, rebuilding self-esteem, and creating a life of authenticity and fulfillment.

By internalizing these lessons and strategies, you are well-equipped to identify and protect yourself from narcissistic abuse in the future. Remember, the self-assessment guide is always available as a resource to help you evaluate the health of your relationships and stay attuned to the warning signs of narcissism.

Embracing a Future Free from Narcissistic Influence

As you move forward with your life, I encourage you to embrace a future that is free from the toxic influence of narcissists. You have the power within you to construct a life that is aligned with your own values and desires, rather than someone else's.

Take care to surround yourself with supportive and empowering people, pursue your passions and goals with vigor, and learn to trust and value yourself in a way that you never have before. But be sure to remain vigilant about spotting the warning signs of toxic behavior in future relationships.

Most importantly, believe in your own inherent worth and resilience, and know that you are capable of overcoming even the darkest of challenges. You are a a beacon of hope and strength for others who may be struggling with similar experiences.

A Call to Action

I now invite you to take the first steps toward your own liberation and empowerment. Start by setting small, achievable goals for yourself, whether that means reaching out to a supportive friend, scheduling a session with a therapist, or simply taking a few moments each day to practice self-care.

As we've said many times, there will be ups and downs along the way. But by staying committed to your own growth and well-being, and by surrounding yourself with love and support, you will find your way to a brighter, more beautiful future.

You are not alone on this path. There is a community of survivors and advocates who are ready to support you and cheer you on every step of the way. And if you ever find yourself in need of further guidance or inspiration, know that there are countless resources available to you, including books, support groups, and online communities dedicated to narcissistic abuse recovery.

A Message of Hope

As a result of your experience, you now have the opportunity to discover your own incredible strength, resilience, and courage. You have the power to rise above the pain of your past and create a future filled with joy, love, and purpose. You are worthy of happiness, respect, and fulfillment, and you have everything you need to make that a reality.

So, take a deep breath, trust in yourself, and know that a beautiful new chapter of your life is waiting to be written. Your freedom starts now, and I am honored to have done what I could to help you along the path to your future.

Stay strong!

Cassandra McBride

References:

American Psychiatric Association. (2013). *Diagnostic and statistical manual of mental disorders* (5th ed.). American Psychiatric Publishing.

Angelou, M. (2008). *Letter to my daughter*. Random House.

Baron-Cohen, S. (2011). *Zero degrees of empathy: A new theory of human cruelty*. Allen Lane.

Bonchay, B. (2018). *Healing from hidden abuse: A journey through the stages of recovery from psychological abuse*. BookBaby.

Brame, A. (2015). The narcissist's addiction: Love bombing. *Psych Central*. https://psychcentral.com/blog/the-narcissists-addiction-love-bombing/

Bremner, J. D. (2006). Traumatic stress. Effects on the brain. *Dialogues in Clinical Neuroscience, 8*(4), 445-461.

Campbell, W. K., & Foster, C. A. (2002). Narcissism and commitment in romantic relationships: An investment model analysis. *Personality and Social Psychology Bulletin, 28*(4), 484-495. https://doi.org/10.1177/0146167202287006

Carnes, P. (2019). *The betrayal bond: Breaking free of exploitive relationships*. Health Communications, Inc.

Durvasula, R. (2018). *Should I stay or should I go?: Surviving a relationship with a narcissist*. Post Hill Press.

Durvasula, R. (2019). *Don't you know who I am?: How to stay sane in an era of narcissism, entitlement, and incivility*. Post Hill Press.

Ettensohn, M. D. (2016). *Unmasking narcissism: A guide to understanding the narcissist in your life.* Althea Press.

Fromm, E. (1956). *The art of loving.* Harper & Row.

Fromm, E. (1964). *The heart of man: Its genius for good and evil.* Harper & Row.

Jung, C. G. (1933). *Modern man in search of a soul* (W. S. Dell & C. F. Baynes, Trans.). Harcourt, Brace & World.

Kant, I. (1785). *Groundwork of the metaphysics of morals* (M. Gregor, Trans.). Cambridge University Press.

Kernberg, O. F. (1975). *Borderline conditions and pathological narcissism.* Jason Aronson.

Kohut, H. (1977). *The restoration of the self.* International Universities Press.

Louis de Canonville, C. (2015). The three phases of narcissistic abuse. *Narcissistic Behavior.* https://narcissisticbehavior.net/the-three-phases-of-narcissistic-abuse/

Machiavelli, N. (1532). *The prince* (W. K. Marriott, Trans.). J. M. Dent & Sons.

Malkin, C. (2015). *Rethinking narcissism: The secret to recognizing and coping with narcissists.* Harper Perennial.

National Coalition Against Domestic Violence. (2021). Statistics. https://ncadv.org/STATISTICS

Northrup, C. (2018). *Dodging energy vampires: An empath's guide to evading relationships that drain you and restoring your health and power.* Hay House, Inc.

Orloff, J. (2017). *The empath's survival guide: Life strategies for sensitive people.* Sounds True.

Payson, E. (2002). *The wizard of Oz and other narcissists: Coping with the one-way relationship in work, love, and family.* Julian Day Publications.

Rand, A. (1964). *The virtue of selfishness.* New American Library.

Sarkis, S. (2018). *Gaslighting: Recognize manipulative and emotionally abusive people—and break free.* Hachette Books.

Schneider, J. P., & Corley, M. D. (2002). Disclosure of extramarital sexual activities by sexually exploitative professionals and other persons with addictive or compulsive sexual disorders. *Journal of Sex Education and Therapy, 27*(2), 109-121.

Stern, R. (2018). *The gaslight effect: How to spot and survive the hidden manipulation others use to control your life.* Harmony Books.

Streep, P. (2016). Narcissism and sexuality: The link between narcissistic personality traits and sexual issues. *Psychology Today.* https://www.psychologytoday.com/us/blog/tech-support/201610/narcissism-and-sexuality

Twenge, J. M., & Campbell, W. K. (2009). *The narcissism epidemic: Living in the age of entitlement.* Simon and Schuster.

Van der Kolk, B. A. (2014). *The body keeps the score: Brain, mind, and body in the healing of trauma.* Penguin Books.

Wilde, O. (1891). *The picture of Dorian Gray.* Ward, Lock and Company.

www.ingramcontent.com/pod-product-compliance
Lightning Source LLC
Chambersburg PA
CBHW071154120626
46546CB00006B/2259